The Diamond Alphabe

The Diamond Alphabet
BASEBALL IN SHORTS

★ GEORGE BOWERING ★

BookThug · 2011

FIRST EDITION
Copyright ©2011 George Bowering

ALL RIGHTS RESERVED

No part of this publication may be reproduced or transmitted in any form or by any means, electronic or mechanical, including photocopying, recording, or any information storage or retrieval system, without permission in writing from the publishers.

Cover image after Matt Dorfman's design for "I Love Dollars," by Zhu Wen, Penguin 2008

The production of this book was made possible through the generous assistance of the Ontario Arts Council and the Canada Council for the Arts.

 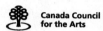

LIBRARY AND ARCHIVES CANADA CATALOGUING IN PUBLICATION

Bowering, George, 1935–
    The diamond alphabet/ George Bowering.

ISBN 978-1-897388-94-5

    1. Baseball – Miscellanea. 2. Alphabet books. I. Title.

GV873.B655 2011   796.357   C2011-904779-9

PRINTED IN CANADA

CONTENTS

A..............................7
B..............................15
C..............................23
D..............................31
E..............................39
F..............................47
G..............................55
H..............................65
I..............................73
J..............................81
K..............................89
L..............................97
M.............................105
N.............................113
O.............................121
P.............................129
Q.............................137
R.............................145
S.............................155
T.............................163
U.............................173
V.............................181
W.............................189
X.............................197
Y.............................205
Z.............................213

This book is for Expressway, Fingers, Popcorn and Fast Eddie,

ANAHEIM

Thea was going on thirteen, and if I didn't get her to Disneyland this year, it would be too late. Fourteen-year-old daughters don't let their fathers take them to Disneyland.

So we waved goodbye to Angela and got into the fairly new Honda and headed south. Aha, the open road, we both shouted, enacting one of our many rituals.

On the way down the I-5, after we got out of the range of the CBC, we managed to tune in a constant run of old fogey stations. Thea managed to sing along quite often, because I had taught her how to sing the standards off-key. "Gee, but it's great, after staying out late."

In San Francisco we stayed in the North Beach motel her mother and I had stayed in twenty years earlier. She was afraid to venture out because of earthquakes and the Zebra Killer.

In Tijuana she wouldn't accept an ice cream cone because her mother had told her to watch what she ate or drank in Mexico. On the way back north we had to wait two hours at the US customs while they hassled the Mexicans and helicopters thudded overhead.

In Anaheim I splurged on a big-name hotel, and in the morning Thea was pissed off when she found out that she could have had eggs benedict instead of the buffet scrambled eggs. Then we went to Disneyland. I was scared of all the rides, what a dad.

Then we went to see the Blue Jays play the Angels. It was a new ballpark for my collection. We got seats down by the left field foul pole, and settled in among the old guys with their transistor radios.

Now, my four favourite things are jazz, beer, Mexican food and baseball. With these old white guys sitting in this theme park stadium, there wasn't going to be any jazz, and the beer, being Bud or Miller, was questionable. But I figured that at least we were right up next to Mexico. The ballpark nachos would not be that stuff we get in Vancouver – some melted Cheez Whiz on triangular chips. I gave Thea a handful of that funny green money and told her to bring me some Southern California nachos, and to pile on the jalapeños.

What did I get? Cheez Whiz melted on triangular chips, and a mountain of sliced jalapeños. I ate the latter.

And I understood Anaheim.

ARTIE

When I went as writer in residence to Sir George Williams University in Montreal in 1967 they made me conduct a creative writing seminar. I think I did it for two years. In one of those classes I had as students Dwight Gardiner and Artie Gold. This was lucky. None of my colleagues in the English department had ever heard of Jack Spicer or Frank O'Hara. But these were the two favourite poets for Dwight and Artie. Dwight and Artie became well-published poets, though they would never be read by the people in the English department of Sir George Williams University.

In 1967 I published a nine-section poem entitled *Baseball*. The book was edited by bpNichol and published by Coach House Press. In the sixties Coach House was infamous for publishing books that were difficult to consume. Sometimes this was because the poems were written by Victor Coleman. Sometimes it was because they were printed in magenta letters on mint-green paper. In the case of *Base-*

ball, the writing wasn't so hard to read. An important character in the text is Jack Spicer, after all.

No, the difficulty in consuming this time had to do with storing the book. It was printed with a green cover that resembled the artificial turf to be found on the playing field of the Houston Astros that year, and the Montreal Expos a few years later. When the book was opened it looked like an elongated diamond, but when it was closed it looked like a triangular pennant. If you put it in your bookshelf among the other new poetry books, it sat on a funny angle, and in little time it would get the pointed end all mushed up. Librarians and book dealers hated it. Collectors cursed my name.

Artie Gold was a famous collector. He collected glass objects, Frank O'Hara broadsheets, agates, Arthur Rakham, Bach recordings, obscure curios, and so on. Wherever he lived looked like a magician's playroom. He didn't know anything about baseball, but he was a twenty-one-year-old expert on poetry. I gave him a copy of my green triangle.

And he knew what to do with it. First he read it. Then he nailed it to the wall with his other pennants.

ASTERISK

We have been hearing about Roger Maris's asterisk for most of the decades in our lives. In that magic summer of 1961 the Berlin Wall went up and Maris and Mickey Mantle went chasing after Babe Ruth's mark of sixty home runs in a single season, the "most honoured record in all of baseball." It so happened that 1961 also saw the American League expand from eight teams to ten, new franchises established in Washington and Los Angeles. Expansion meant that the schedule had to include 162 games rather than 154.

So when Mantle and Maris went on a home run tear late in the season, the sentimentalist crowd began to fear for the Babe's pre-eminence. One of the sentimentalists was Ford Frick, the Commissioner of Baseball at the time. Frick was a good pal of Ruth, and in fact wrote most of the newspaper and magazine articles published above Ruth's name during his career. So when Roger Maris spurted past Mantle, and registered his 61st homer in the Yankees' 162nd game, Commissioner Ford had an asterisk placed beside his total in the official record book.

It's the most famous asterisk in sports. But it never existed. The famous asterisk is only a symbol that appears time and again, as when the guy that owned some famous Barry Bonds home run ball said that he was going to brand a big asterisk in it. Maris's total of 61 has been passed numerous times, by three National League hitters juiced with steroids. He still owns the American League record, and some observers say that he should have an asterisk beside his name, indicating the only player to hit 61 home runs without chemical help.

The idea that Maris should have carried an asterisk because he had eight more games than did Ruth is pretty questionable. Don't bring up the question of expansion rotations – only one of the homers came off a pitcher new to the league. And don't listen to the smart guys that wanted Ichiro Suzuki to acquire an asterisk for his new total of 262 base hits in 2004. A lot of records have been set since 1961, and even since the Berlin Wall came down.

George Herman Ruth hit lots of late-inning homers off starting pitchers who were not, in the twenties, removed for fresh arms after a hundred pitches. He never had to bat against African-American or Latino chuckers or guys with a great circle change. He didn't have to hit under the lights and then in a park across the country the next night. The pitchers in 1927 were, on average, shorter and lighter than the pitchers decades later. Outfielders who leapt up against the fence to try to grab sure shots did not have gloves the size of suitcases. Maybe Babe Ruth should have had an asterisk.

AUGIE

Back in the day, when the Cecil Hotel was the weekly drinking pub for writers, before some sideburned guys from Surrey put in carpet-ting and turned it into a strip joint, David Alguire used to sit in, a true friend who did not happen to be a poet or novelist, at least I don't think he was. He was also a valiant worker in the underground press.

Then he moved back to Toronto, where he got a job as a landscaper with the city. In the eighties, when I went to Toronto to do a reading or two, I could depend on Jamie Reid and Augie to be friends in the audience. I really like a person such as Augie, a guy who keeps tabs on the poetry scene without having to be a poet himself.

Every year now, Augie comes to Vancouver for his annual vacation in August. He always has a terrific tan due to the fact that he has been working outdoors ever since the snow disappeared. Augie is a good friend of the poet George Stanley, who is a good friend of mine, and has in fact lived in my house twice. So every August, George and Augie and I, and probably my wife Jean and maybe George's brother Gerald, go to Nat Bailey Stadium when the Canadians are on a homestand.

Every year we take pictures of us in the stands, sometimes grinning, sometimes doing the Sixth Inning Chicken Dance, occasionally grasping plastic cups of beer. In a recent snap I am wearing my San Francisco Giants cap, George is wearing a Vancouver Canadians cap, and Augie is wearing what he always wears. Augie doesn't wear a cap, even under the brightest sun. He has dirty blond hair that passes through a rubber band and hangs down his back to his waist. And every time he goes to a baseball game in Vancouver he wears the tee shirt he got at Nat Bailey Stadium a decade ago. It proclaims that the Vancouver Canadians were the Division Champions. Augie is a Toronto Vancouver Canadians fan for sure.

I think it is the same way he is a poetry fan. It is unlikely, I would venture to say, that he knows who Johnnie Logan played for. He probably couldn't give you a title from the works of Lorene Niedecker. But I like going to baseball games with Augie, and I like it when he comes to a poetry reading.

AUSTRALIA

One of the worst periods of our life was the 232 days between August 12, 1994 and April 2, 1995. The major league players went on strike because the team owners wanted to institute revenue sharing and a salary cap. The millionaire players thought they were going to be screwed by the millionaire owners. Of course the National Basketball Association has a salary cap, and it has actually brought the owners and players together: the owners finagle the books to get under the salary cap and pay the players thousands of dollars a dribble.

This was the fourth strike action in 23 years. The kid's dream of baseball as an alternative world was just about shattered. The morning newspaper was just about a pointless experience without the box scores. There was no post-season play in 1994. When play, I mean work, ended, the Montreal Expos had the best record and the best outfield in baseball. They were slated to face the Yankees in the World Series and beat them. We Expos fans had been simmering with excitement for weeks and weeks.

When the world stopped, I think a lot of Expos fans suspected that the US American players and owners had got together to put the kibosh on a Montreal championship.

In February of 1995 I went to Melbourne for a conference on Canadian studies. One of the things I had to do was sit on a panel about sports, with Alan Lawson, the Australian professor and rugby enthusiast, and Brian Edwards, Australian professor and golfer/fisherman, and Alison Gordon, the dandy Toronto crime fiction author. Alison used to be a baseball reporter, covering the Blue Jays for the Toronto *Star*. Then she wrote a series of murder mysteries with a female baseball reporter as amateur detective. Mystery writers look for snazzy titles, and Alison started with one of the all-time best: *The Dead Pull Hitter*.

Alison was feeling the loss of the postseason, too, and when we found out that Melbourne's ball team the Waverley Reds were playing in the semi-final playoff against the Sydney Blues, we persuaded the wonderful Beryl Langer, Australian expert on North American popular culture, to drive us to the ball park. No one knew where the stadium was.

"Look for lights in the sky," I said. "I've done this lots of times."

We drove and drove around Melbourne, and saw the lights in the sky, and arrived in time for the bottom of the 7th inning. Alison was ecstatic. Her husband Paul bought her a hotdog and a beautiful red teeshirt with an image of some animal eating a baseball bat. Our Reds won 7–4 and advanced to the Australian World Series. I don't know how Alison felt about the Sydney uniforms – they were modelled after the Blue Jays uniforms, with those modernistic letters and numbers.

Next day we all went to the beach and had a game of beach cricket. Alison sat in a beach chair, so I whacked two pitches in a row past her head. I was trying to impress the baseball writer with my bat control.

BABE

Before they built the new Oliver Theatre on Main Street, we went to see movies in the Legion Hall. We would sit on two-by-twelves resting on upturned apple boxes, and listen to the projector laying out our western or our Disney. For a while after they opened the new Oliver Theatre, across the side road and on Main Street too, both places showed movies.

On Saturdays most of the boys went to the new Oliver Theatre with the folding padded seats and the projector you could hear only during the really quiet and suspenseful scenes. And because they did, I preferred to go to the Legion.

Most of those boys preferred Roy Rogers, so I preferred Gene Autry. Champion rather than Trigger. No one rather than Dale. "Back in the Saddle Again" rather than "Happy Trails to You."

Most of those boys liked to see Lash LaRue, but I held out for the underdog Whip Wilson. Looking back, I might have chosen the former because he was Cajun, but I just thought he was trying to be fawncy with a French name.

Those boys chose Superman with his up up and away business, so of course I became a Batman fan. Har dee har, they said, he hasn't even got any superpowers. Exactly, I replied, trying to sound mysteriously wise.

15

Here we were in a little podunk in the far west of Canada, and those boys were all New York Yankees followers. Not I. I became a Red Sox fan at the age of ten.

So I extolled the fiery and aloof Ted Williams, while they were all of them gaga for Joe DiMaggio.

And when it came to the all-time history of our great game, I held out for the little-known Ty Cobb while they all confidently announced the eminence of Babe Ruth.

BASEBALLS

There are baseballs here and there in our house, and a few in the garage. Even after taking a bunch of them to give away in Cuba last year, I have enough of them to last the rest of my life, especially considering that I retired from the diamond after I broke my hip five years ago. Some of them are souvenirs, such as the first pitch I threw to Damian Miller in Miller Park a couple springs ago.

I used to buy pieces of Depression glass in second-hand stores, so on top of our bedroom bookshelf I have a bowl of baseballs. It kind of looks like a Cézanne still-life. The balls are all white. Most of the baseballs in my house are white. The ones in the garage and yard are brown, like the baseballs I had when I was a kid.

When I was a kid you never got to play with a white baseball or infield grass, and you certainly never had a new white baseball at home. The closest you came to a white baseball was when you chased foul balls behind the Oliver grandstand and brought them in for ten cents apiece, and they weren't really white anymore. Sometimes when you were looking for them in the long wet grass under the big irrigation siphon, you would find a muggy old ball from the previous summer. That's what you played catch with.

Quite often when I stop to think about something in our house I reach out and pick up a baseball. Doesn't it fit the hand nicely, two fingers over the red seams, arm hanging loose or hand behind your ear as if you were a catcher? How can a person run eighty feet and jump up against a high fence and catch this little thing? How does he know exactly where to go to get it? And given its perfect whiteness and the feel of those seams, how can he throw it away?

When I was a kid I used to look forward to adulthood, when I would be able to buy an ice cream cone any time I wanted to. And someday I would have my own brand new pure white horsehide, even though they might make them out of cowhide in Haiti or China. Now I have lots of baseballs around, and I didn't buy any of them. Somehow they settle in our house, and I pick one up and sniff it and feel it with my thumb, and if Lionel Kearns arrives with his old glove I get a brown one from the garage and we go and play catch.

BOISE

More often than not, the Boise Hawks finish first in the eastern division of the Northwest League. The most distantly separated teams in the Northwest League are the Boise Hawks and the Vancouver Canadians, and there is a big difference in climate between Nat Bailey Stadium and Campbell Memorial Stadium.

If you go to a game at Campbell Memorial Stadium on July 17th the temperature at game time against the Eugene Emeralds will be 102 degrees. The seats along the third base line cost more than all the others because for an hour, maybe, you might get some shade. Still, this is better than being back at the hotel where the air conditioning is not working and two East Indian guys are trying to fix it, but it isn't going to work.

Downtown there is a big square surrounded by high-rise office buildings, and in that square there is an open fountain with water jetting straight up for three or four meters. People walk through the fountain, knowing that their clothes will be dry again in fifteen minutes. What an intelligent thing to do with your downtown!

The Hawks are a Short Season/ Single-A team in the Chicago

Cubs system, but they have to employ a designated hitter because three of the teams in the league are American League farms. At least they don't have to wear white shoes as the Vancouver Canadians do just because they are in the Oakland system.

When it gets to about the sixth inning in Campbell Memorial Stadium, you remember those hundred-degree afternoons in the Okanagan Valley when uniforms were woolen, including your high stirrups, and you feel sorry for the home plate umpire with the chest-protector who does not get to spend half the game in the shadow of the dugout, and you would still rather be here than in an air-conditioned den watching the Royals and Twins on television.

Here in the state in which Ezra Pound was born and Ernest Hemingway died, we think about Modernism a little, although mostly we cheer for the home team, but for the second time in eleven days, we watch the Eugene Emeralds score in the top of the ninth inning and win, this time 6–4.

BOUDREAU

In 1948, the greatest year in the history of civilization, I was twelve years old all during the baseball season, and I had been a Boston Red Sox fan all my life, or rather since 1946. Intelligent twelve-year-olds are the most fervent baseball fans, and things were exciting in my family because my dad was a Cleveland Indians fan. Well, the Indians were very interesting that year, and when I think back I can remember at least as many of the 1948 Indians as I can the Red Sox.

You know what happened. The Red Sox and Indians finished in a tie, with the Yankees two games back. Then in the league's first ever one-game playoff, Indians player-manager Lou Boudreau went 4 for 4 with a walk at Fenway Park to win the pennant for Cleveland. A week later the Indians would be back in Boston, finishing off the Braves for the World Series victory.

Early in the season Bill Veeck had tried to trade Boudreau to the

Browns, but the whole city of Cleveland rose up in anger to prevent the deal, and 155 games later Boudreau finished the season batting .355, second to Ted Williams, with a .497 on-base percentage, second to Williams, .534 slugging average, fourth behind Williams, and a .987 OPS, third after Williams and Joe DiMaggio. He was by far the hardest AL hitter to strike out, and he was voted the league's Most Valuable Player.

My father smiled a lot while reading the sports page of the Vancouver *Sun* that summer and fall. I was spending all my earnings on sports magazines, and memorizing pictures of Gene Beardon, Ken Keltner – and Lou Boudreau. There were a lot of pictures of Lou Boudreau, and as I looked at them that winter I tried to hate him, but I couldn't.

My best buddy Bill Lyttle didn't know anything about baseball or any other sport, but he picked up stuff from me because I wouldn't shut up about it. He even helped me invent new sports such as economical ball and telephone wire tennis. The latter used, instead of a ball, the little round carton that had contained fixer for our basement darkroom. Many of the pictures we developed owed their inspiration to the 1948 American League pennant race.

We had noticed that many if not most of the pictures of Lou Boudreau that showed up in *Sport* or *Sports Life* showed him looking upward. So for two years a lot of the pictures we took of each other showed Bill sitting on a rock with his winter coat on, his eyes looking upward, or me standing beside a pine tree, an ugly hat on my head and my eyes directed skyward. Now whenever anyone mentions the 1948 playoff American League game, I groan and cast my gaze toward Heaven.

BOWSFIELD

In the latter part of the 1958 season pitcher Ted Bowsfield was brought up from Minneapolis to become a starter for the Boston Red Sox. The

Yankees would run away with the 1958 pennant and best Milwaukee in the World Series, but 23-year-old Bowsfield beat them on August 10, August 15 and September 1 on his way to a 4–2 record with a 3.80 ERA.

Bowsfield was born in Vernon and went to high school in Penticton, and his middle name is Oliver. I went to high school in Oliver and I was born in Penticton, but my middle name is Harry. So much for that connection. Except that my last name comes just before his in any theoretical record of junior baseball players in the Okanagan Valley.

You see what precarious connections we old baseball fans hang onto when it comes to how far we were from the show? And, consequently, how shifty our memories are? I do remember sitting at the scorer's table in the Penticton High School gymnasium (I just now Googled that gym and found a picture of it's being torn down four months ago) keeping a sharp record of a senior boys' basketball game between the Southern Okanagan High School Green Hornets and the Penticton High Lakers. Ted Bowsfield was a muscular 6 foot 3 inch forward for the home team.

I'm sure that I scored some baseball games he pitched in, too. But did I ever play against him? In the first place, I didn't play a lot of organized baseball when I was a kid. I played some with the Oliver juniors and some with the Naramata juniors, in those last beautiful years before Little League came in and ruined childhood.

Here's a memory I might have and might not have. I came in to pinch hit late in a game against Penticton, and Bowsfield was throwing one of his usual games of alternating strikeouts and walks. God, he was big up there on that high mound! His first pitch toward me hit the backstop screen about eight feet up. I think I hit the dirt anyway. I stood up and found a place as far back and as far to my left as I could find in the batter's box. This was in the days before batting helmets, too. When I heard ball four go by I was never so glad to head for first base. I ran all the way.

Here's another memory. It was my first game ever as a junior, in my last year of eligibility, and I came up to bat in the first inning with the bases loaded. Knowing myself better than anyone else could, I expected to strike out, but I managed a single to the right side of second base, and my first ever RBI. I always like to tell myself that I got that single off Ted Bowsfield, but I doubt it.

CBL

When the Canadian Baseball League was announced early in the Twenty-First Century, I could not believe my luck. We were living in the peculiar little town of Port Colborne, Ontario, and one of the teams in the eastern division of the CBL would be the Niagara Stars. The Stars would play their home games in Welland, Ontario, about twenty minutes up a back highway.

Someone told someone in the press somewhere that the CBL would be equivalent to Double-A baseball in the big scheme of things. Well, yeah, uh-huh, we said – but I have to admit that I got a little excited. Imagine – having a home team in a professional baseball league, with the drive so short and the parking so free! And then they came looking for me!

Well, no, not as a back-up second baseman. I was at the time writing a book titled *Baseball Love*, and I was a little bit known as a baseball fan. On top of that I had been recently recruited as the first Canadian Parliamentary poet laureate. It had to be worth something, eh? I was invited to throw out the first ball for the Niagara Stars' second home game. The first game ceremony was going to be taken care of by the league's commissioner, Ferguson Jenkins, who grew up in Ontario before going to live in Oklahoma.

But the home opener was rained out. We sat in our car among

the growing puddles in the dirt parking lot, trying to think of something else to do in Welland. Then we heard the good news – Fergie couldn't hang around for the next day's game, so I got to throw out the first ever first ball in Welland Stars history. And so I did, a strike on the inside corner, according to the catcher, Rogelio Arias from Villa Duarte, Dominican Republic. He signed the ball for me, as first-ball catchers traditionally do, and I still have it, in the bowl of baseballs on our bedroom windowsill. I have thrown out the first ball four times, and I still have three of them.

Then things got even better. I was interviewed while standing at the screen, with the ballgame going on behind me, by The Score, the national sports network that had signed to carry the CBL's games. I got so much sidetracked by that camera and all the rest, that I cannot remember now who won that game. I think that the London Monarchs did. But the Stars had the best player name. This belonged to second baseman Toby Legacy, and he was a Canadian!

The CBL drew decent crowds in Victoria and Calgary, but the Montreal team couldn't even find a place to play in Montreal, and the other teams couldn't draw flies. Our Stars finished 15–15, and after the all-star game in Calgary, the owners folded the league "temporarily." At that all-star game, they held a home run contest, but no one could hit a home run. Sometimes you have to be friendly with irony to be a Canadian.

CHICAGO

If your sweetheart lives in Port Colborne, Ontario, and you live in Vancouver, BC, you tend to get into airplanes often. One way to meet is to converge on Chicago, and if I may focus a little, sit together during the daytime at Wrigley Field.

Jean drove to Buffalo and flew from there. The day before that I drove to Seattle and watched the San Francisco game that night.

Barry Bonds came to bat five times and did not run fast toward first base once. I stayed overnight and flew from Seatac the next day.

When I got off the plane in Chicago I was green of face and sick as an old dog, so I did not look out the window of the cab all the way into town, my head on my poor sweetheart's lap. When we got to the hotel I thought I might have ruined yet another day with this being sick business, but we found a way to make me better.

It was a rainy day in midsummer, and I was disconsolate. All my life I have waited to go to Wrigley Park and now it's raining, I whimpered. But we saw ginks in Cub hats and Cub shirts heading for the El, so we tagged along. It's going to be pouring rain, I mewled, and my whole trip is ruined. My darling said "ahem" and I backtracked. And sure enough it quit raining and a big midwestern blue sky was all at once above us, and we walked up the beat-up dirty old outfield ramp, and there we were, in the right-centre field bleachers!

It was still humid after the rain, and the sun beat on us, bleaching our brains. To counteract it, I bought us a couple of big drinks, but first I got advice. Why, I asked the two tattooed bikers with long greasy hair beside us, are you guys drinking mai-tais? Because, they instructed me, the beer is four dollars and the mai-tais are four dollars and they come in the same-sized cups.

Learning how to drink in Illinois, we enjoyed the party known as the Wrigley bleachers. People joked with strangers, passed their popcorn down the rows, sang bawdy songs, and paid a kid greenbacks. This kid had a hand-held battery-powered fan that could spray cold water in your face. I think that Wrigley should never be replaced by a modern structure with skyboxes. It is the site of good old baseball such as your grandfather sighed about.

COOPERSTOWN

I'm sure that dads take their sons to the Hall of Fame, hoping that they will get all moony-eyed about Hank Greenberg or maybe Ernie

Banks. But there are two places where you can be sure to find those boys – in front of one of the television sets, or in the gift shop. They might even be looking down at their cell phones.

I did not get to see a major league baseball game till I was thirty years old, and I did not get to visit the Hall of Fame till Bob Hogg's fiftieth birthday. I went there in a little rented car after a poetry-reading trip of New England and upper New York State. The library was closed because it was being relocated. What a nuisance. But I got to see the plaque for Heinie Manush, BA .330, OPS .856. I bought a Heinie Manush postcard. I hardly ever buy clothes, but here I was in the Hall of Fame, eh? It was a year before Colorado and Florida got into the National League. Would I get teal or purple? I got a Colorado Rockies jacket, and I was still wearing it yesterday.

There, I said to my lonely self, the self I persuade myself in such circumstances, I like best, there – I have seen the Parthenon and the Baseball Hall of Fame. The abode where the Eternal are. Fame, said Shelley, is love deferred. When I get to Heaven I'm going to get Heinie Manush's autograph.

My friend Stan used to go to Cooperstown to listen to classical chamber music, and never went into a building containing a baseball. He and I both walked down to the waterfront to admire the old colonial lake. The second time I visited the place where baseball was not invented, my sweetheart Jean and I arrived in a small rented car and found the last motel room right down by the lake, an old traditional wooden place with oft-painted window frames.

The Hall of Fame, as usually happens, did not much resemble my memory of it. But I found my way into the room full of plaques and stood in front of Johnny Evers, and as I have all my sensible life, wondered what he is doing in the Hall of Fame. BA .270, SLG .334. He may have been necessary for a song, but if you get into the Hall of Fame because of a song, where is Dom DiMaggio?

I have always held to the opinion that baseball fans are more intelligent and cultured than the fans of hockey and basketball. I like to hearken back to the days when we still had Triple-A baseball in Vancouver, through the eighties and nineties. My friends and I – poets, students, professors, journalists, union negotiators – would sit in sunny Section 9 and discuss baseball, once in a while making vocal assessments of the game and players we were watching.

There was a visiting baseball fellow – I think that he toiled for the Tucson Toros – named Poochie Delgado. When Poochie came to the plate my friends and I would greet him with sounds we thought appropriate. "Woof woof!" we would say. "Arf arf!" Then we would smile our secret smiles at one another. It was very pleasant to be seated with your intellectual buddies at a ball game on a July evening.

There was another Toro we liked to make sound effects for. I can't recall his name, but will never forget his batting stance. He would spread his feet far apart, and then do a kind of squat, bouncing up and down as he awaited the pitch. When he did this, my learned friends and I made the kind of sound you get if you squeeze your lips together and blow out your breath. Section 9 at Nat Bailey Stadium is not far from the action on the field, and we were certain that this feigned flatulence reached Tucson ears.

We know that we could be heard by Manny Estrada. Manny Estrada was a power hitter for the Spokane Indians, a person who hit a double and a homer on his first visit to Nat Bailey Stadium. But he stayed in the Pacific Coast League for year after year because when major league general managers looked at his stats they saw that he was about five and a half feet tall. This physical characteristic was our cue. "It's a game of inches, Manny!" we would shout. "Hit a short-hopper!" we would enjoin him. Once he was part of a conference on the mound. "Hey, you can see a lot from up there, eh, Manny?" I hollered. He turned and waggled his hand open and shut toward us, proving that he could hear every word.

So when Brad "The Animal" Lesley was sent down to pitch in the PCL for a while, we loudly referred to him as "The Vegetable." When Dale Sveam, the dullest ballplayer in the Milwaukee system, played third base for the Canadians, we dubbed him "Mister Colour."

But our favourite games were those in which a visiting player named Cox came to town. I can't remember his first name or his affiliation, but I remember joining my brain trust in riffing on his surname. "Let's get Cox out," we would encourage our defensive team. "We want to see Cox pop up," we would inform our pitcher.

We constituted the avant-garde in the field of baseball cheering.

CUBA

If you are anywhere near the big square under the trees in downtown Havana in the late afternoon or in the evening, you will see a lot of men and older boys standing in a crowd and disputing animatedly. In a lot of places the subject might be religion or politics. Here in the *Parque Central* they are arguing about baseball. That moronic manager Rey Anglada was acting only out of sentimentality to leave old Norge Luis Vera in after Santiago tied the game off him. Aw, you are too young, you have no understanding of how great Norge Luis has been for thirteen years.

What fun to walk into this crowd, then, and listen to all the wisdom shared in that very fast way the Cubans talk, and then to reach into your bag and start handing out baseball cards and pins and magazines and baseballs. Name ought to be Hemingway. Ought to be Thank You, it is such a privilege to be under these trees sharing baseball stuff. There goes the last of my John Kruk cards.

There were twenty-six of us, twenty-eight counting Ernesto our driver and Clem our facilitator, wearing Cuban ball caps and riding the air-conditioned Chinese bus, dropping in to see games in Pinar del Rio or Cienfuegos. It's a dream baseball trip come true, and it's even more marvelous because in the afternoon you get to see the *Granma,* a boat far more famous than the *Maine,* and then that night you go to the big Latin America Stadium and root for the underdog Metropolitans in their red caps against the blue-capped Industriales, cheered for by 49,000 of the 50,000 people in the stands.

Wearing my red cap with the M on the front of it, I lost my voice and my senses as an amazingly beautiful game was played in front of me, no advertisements on the fences, a warm February night filled with loud revolutionary baseball cheering. The Metropolitans scored a tying run on a balk. A Metropolitan caught up to a fly ball at the center field fence and threw the runner out at the plate. Double play! With two out in the bottom of the ninth, the Metropolitans got three straight hits to defeat their crosstown rivals 6–5. I proudly sported my red cap as I joined the stream of Cubanos out of the park.

Later that night at an outdoor restaurant in Havana Antigua I sat with Jean and enjoyed some superb flounder. In Cuba the baseball is better than any other, the food is nothing to write home about, but if you can find a place that offers fish pulled from the Caribbean, take off your Metropolitans cap, sit down, and tuck in. There will be someone there with music any moment.

DH

I wasn't even around then, but I am nostalgic for the days when the boys on your university football team played the whole game. After you scored a touchdown or gave up the ball by punting, you took up your position on defence. You could probably see some trees from the football field, too. Then for some reason along came the offensive team, the defensive team and the special teams that make up a football squad in the commercialized murderized National Football League we have today.

Okay, let them have football, I say. But they should stay away from baseball, the football types. Once in a while at a baseball game you see a clot of drunken young men pouring beer on their neighbours and shouting sexist and homophobic remarks, and you know that these are football fans who have invaded *your* house.

It's people like that who invented the designated hitter. If you thought that the sacrifice fly rule was a crock, you were really browned off by the designated hitter. Oh no, you said, I don't want to see my game footballized. If a designated hitter, why not a designated runner? How about we go all the way and have a defensive squad and an offensive squad? We could have a defensive coordinator.

Who was the idiot that started the DH? Did he not notice that baseball is by nature a defensive game? It is the only major game I know in which the defence puts the ball into play. It is telling that it was the American League that started this nonsense. One always knew that the American League was for the kind of fan that was not in favour of thinking, the kind of fan who would prefer the Yankees to, say, the Cardinals, Murderers' Row to the Gas House Gang.

The DH is loved by the muscleheads who think a pitchers' duel is boring. They are a little like Englishmen who think that baseball is "slow." The DH crowd says that we want more scoring, more fireworks, more noise – that we do not want a scoreless game in extra innings. They say that people will be turned off baseball if there aren't enough three-run homers. Well, soccer is the most popular team sport in the world, and a typical score is 1–0.

DODGERS

When I was a lad there were a lot of movies about the US Americans winning the Second World War. The usual structure involved seeing a platoon of young GIs from recruitment all the way to the final battle. They were a representative bunch. There was a guy who read books and might wear glasses. He was called "Professor." There was a dumb guy from Texas, an older guy who kept to himself, and a little guy from Brooklyn. The little guy from Brooklyn was sure to die on the ground, but before he did he would ask the other guys how the Dodgers had done the night before.

I have been to New York City a number of times, and I have visited every borough but Brooklyn. Since 1958, when the Bums moved to Los Angeles, there has been no reason to go to Brooklyn. Well, if I ever get there during the middle of the summer – but then who in his right mind wants to go to that humidity in the summer? – I might go and see the Single-A Brooklyn Cyclones, though I am still browned off that they left St Catharines, Ontario.

What I am trying to say is that I have been a Dodgers fan all my life, and even went to Chavez Ravine to see them a few years back. I was one of the few people who got there before the first pitch and did not leave till after the last pitch. When I was a kid I was nuts for Jackie Robinson and Duke Snider and Peewee Reese and Don Newcombe. And I was a traditionalist, a conservative. I would like the socialist hordes to take over the United States, but when it comes to baseball I am a conservative. So I knew that something was going wrong when they put *red* numbers on the *front* of the Dodgers' uniforms.

I mean, come on! The Dodgers get African Americans back into big league baseball, thus announcing that the US might catch up to Cuba and Mexico when it comes to social reform in sports – and then they put red numbers on the front of the shirt. What next, I asked, when I was fifteen – will they go for white shoes? Coloured tops? Pre-curled cap visors? It was enough to make a person a Giants fan. Wait, no. My father was a Giants fan.

My father never saw the Giants play, in New York or San Francisco, or anywhere. I have never been to Brooklyn, and when I was a kid I never dodged a trolley. Willard Mullin's cartoon of a bum with a cigar stub spoke to me. He was from the big city and I was a kid with home-made shirts in the dry valley village, but I sharpened my second-hand spikes just the way Eddie Stanky did.

DOGS

One day my chums and I walked up to a ball game at Memorial Stadium in Everett, and noticed that one of the people headed for the yard was holding a leash with a Dalmatian at the end of it. Then we saw a guy with a Black Lab. Then a woman with a Fox Terrier. Pretty soon we were surrounded by mutts and purebreds as we bought our tickets for the first base side. To get to the first base side we had to walk past all the hotdog and souvenir booths. Some of the booths were offering cans of dog food. Then we saw a sign that offered "free Frisbees for the first 1000 dogs." We saw some dogs chasing their new Frisbees through the sky in the field back of the stadium.

It was our first ever Bark in the Park. After the fifth inning there was a grand parade of the dogs, about a hundred of them, in a line that skirted the infield. We did not see one dog or owner squatting. In the middle of the seventh inning there was a great Frisbee-catching exhibition by Cecil the Wonder Dog or some such creature. It wasn't as much fun as the great Trout Toss in Missoula, but it was pretty good.

Now there are Barks in the Park at ballgames all over the continent. We saw one in Toledo that was pretty lame. There were about ten dogs in the parade. One of them was a Harlequin Great Dane, though. That was something. The dumbest one we have seen was in Vancouver. You could bring your dog, all right, but there was no parade, and no free bones or anything. All the dogs that did attend had to stay leashed and sit down around their humans' feet. It's a good thing that they use wooden bats in pro baseball – when Max's dog would hear the metal bat hitting a baseball at the University of British Columbia games, she would start howling like a coyote.

Nat Bailey Stadium in Vancouver used to be the stage for a black dog named Baseball Sam, though. Baseball Sam would come out after the sixth inning and make amazing Frisbee jump-catches. My friends and I in Section 9 would always shout, "Get that dog off the field!"

Vancouver was also the site of the Kozmik League, the theatrical organization that explored the interface of sport, poetry and circus. One of the KL rules was that like umpires, all dogs were in play. This was a necessary regulation because many of the KL players were superannuated hippies, and hippies always went around with animals that were partly German Shepherds. As shortstop for the Granville Grange Zephyrs I once started a double play with a ball that had bounced off a Standard Poodle.

DONKEYS

You could pile up a lot of great memories while growing up in a hot dry valley 250 miles and a couple of mountain ranges from Vancouver and the rest of the Coast. A lot of them had to do with the baseball park with its rickety old grandstand down across the river. Normally there was the Okanagan Mainline Baseball League, with its games on Saturdays, and then when everyone got a little less religious, on Sundays. When I was really young there was the kind of softball called fastball, with my dad as the catcher for the Oliver Elks. Then there was the baseball league that included teams from towns up and down the Okanagan Valley on both sides of the 49th Parallel. Kelowna, British Columbia and Omak, Washington, for example. Then for reasons I never learned, we had the eight-team all-Canadian OMBL, that stretched from Kamloops in the north to Trail in the southeast.

Eight teams, just like the two major leagues. In other words, real. If the major leagues ever changed from eight teams to something less or more, they would not be exactly real any more.

But in addition to league play there were the visitations of trick teams. I scorned them but I would never miss them. A barnstorming team of US Negroes (remember, this was in the late Forties) came to town, and I saw my first ever Black man up close. He had bloodshot eyes, and I took it for granted that all Negroes had bloodshot eyes. But then I wondered, because my many pictures of Jackie Robinson and Larry Doby didn't show me any such thing.

These trick teams would always take on the locals, of course. One group was made up of guys with long beards. They called themselves the House of David. I had no idea what that could possibly mean, who David was, why a House? Of course, I could have asked one of them, but I was not the sort of boy who could work up the nerve to do such a thing. Then there was Eddie Feigner, the King and his Court. He was from just south of us, in Walla Walla, and he was the greatest softball pitcher in history. His team was made of four guys, and he would strike out your best hitters from second base. They were the Globe Trotters of the diamond.

But the goofiest barnstormers were the donkey baseball guys. In a donkey baseball game the outfielders all have donkeys and the offensive team has donkeys. If an outfielder has to chase a ball down he has to do it on donkey back. A hitter has to hop onto the back of his donkey to get down to first, and if he makes it, he is a base runner with an animal. Of course these barnstorming donkeys have all been trained to have certain personalities. There's Wrong Way Corrigan, who wants to head for third instead of first. There's the guy who will not move, no matter how animated you become on his back. There's the one that sits down on his bum and won't get up again. I guess you could say that they are a lot like the Washington Nationals.

DROPO

There have been a lot of nifty names in baseball. In the early Seventies, for example, Walt "No-Neck" Williams and Larvell "Sugar Bear" Blanks, took care of business in Atlanta and Cleveland. In 1992 we went to a Junior Mariners game in Bellingham, and saw young Arquimedez Pozo in a game against the visiting Boise Hawks, who were employing Elgin Bobo. We shouted our enthusiastic support for both youngsters. Unfortunately, Pozo got into only twenty-five major league games, and Bobo got into none at all.

But when I was a boy and a Red Sox fanatic, I was mesmerized by big Walt Dropo, the huge Bosnian-American first baseman who had a spectacular rookie year in 1950, when I was fourteen and madly in love with baseball. In 1951 he broke his wrist, and put the kibosh on what should have been a hall of fame career. In a time when the average major leaguer was about five-foot nine, Dropo was a giant. He was six-foot five and weighed in at 225 pounds – in other words he looked like a twenty-first century ballplayer. They tried to call him "Moose," but it didn't work as it did for Moose Skowron or Elmer "Moose" Vasco.

The name Dropo is not the name Williams. I couldn't find any by using White Pages Canada. Most of the ones I found in the USA are in Massachusetts and Connecticut – including Walt, who is 86 years old as of last month.

But Dropo does show up in made-up stories. There is a pretty important character named Mr Dropo in my YA novel, *Parents from Space*, He is a quality control officer for Barney's Meats. He is always giving his pocket change to the kids. In a 1964 movie called *Santa Claus Conquers the Martians*, or as it was retitled when it came out on video, *Santa Claus Defeats the Aliens*, there is a character named Dropo who is accused of being the "laziest man on Mars." He is played by Bill McCutcheon, who later had roles in *Vibes: the Secret of the Golden Pyramids* and *Mr. Destiny*.

It appears that Dropo is also a village in Cote d'Ivoire and a computer virus that attacks Microsoft Excel.

But for me Walt Dropo will always be my favourite baseball name from the middle of the twentieth century. Try saying it aloud a few times. I think you will hear what I mean.

ENGLAND

Like a lot of good things – Shakespearian sonnets, fish and chips, Morris Minors, Bass Ale – baseball had its origin in England. Most people remember all the Yankee stories about Abner Doubleday inventing the game in a field near Cooperstown in 1839. Doubleday may have fired the first Union shot of the Civil War, and he may have owned the patent for the San Francisco cable cars, but he never claimed to have invented baseball.

Since that upstate New York myth was allowed to fade away, there have been a lot of first baseball games in the northeastern quadrant of the United States, and we have descriptions of games played in Ontario in the mid-thirties, and references to games called "bat" or "ball" going back at least to 1803 in Nova Scotia and elsewhere.

So I have been for a long time sick of the snips, especially the Anglophiles among them, who complain of my being interested in an "American" game instead of, I don't know, soccer, ice hockey, lacrosse, maybe. In the years after they lost the War of 1812, a lot of Americans came and settled in Ontario, some wanting to escape the US, others hoping that Ontario would wise up and join the US. Sure, they brought their versions of "town ball" north with them. But there were already ball games on this side of the line, and they had developed from games brought from England and Wales. A lot of the ball games in New York and Ohio were similarly descended from English sports.

There are stick-and-ball games all over the world, but I can recall Brit immigrants saying, on seeing baseball, that it is really their game of rounders, which some of them went on to call a girl's game. Others would suggest that their polite game cricket had been a victim of savage devolvement after being brought to the wilds of North America.

But baseball is native to Britain, and it was called baseball, or "base ball." It is still being played in Liverpool, Cardiff, Newport and other places on the western side of the country. An early sportswriter named Jane Austen refers to children playing "base-ball" in her novel *Northanger Abbey*, which she finished writing in 1803. Her central character is apparently a woman more interested in sports than in Miss Austen's activity: "It was not very wonderful that Catherine, who had by nature nothing heroic about her, should prefer cricket, baseball, riding on horseback, and running around the country at the age of fourteen, to books." There are plenty of other written references of a less literary kind dating back at least to 1748. In the English game one still sees posts rather than bags to mark the bases, just as in New York in the 1820s.

The English game is fun to watch. It appears to be something between rounders and cricket, or maybe this: our game as it was played when Jane Austen and William Wordsworth were preparing another great English export.

ENOS

My friend Jack Cardoso is the grumpiest baseball fan in the state of New York, and a lifelong St Louis Cardinals fan. I think he was a boyhood friend of Ducky Medwick. Jack claims to have been employed as a professor by some university in Buffalo before he retired or was eased out. Now he is a collector and user of golf equipment and a freelance historian. I like him a lot. He was the first person to take me to the Anchor Grill for Buffalo wings. A while back Jack saw a dream come true when he was assigned to write a historical entry on an old-time Redbird outfielder. He sent me a report of his research.

"I was driving back to NY after checking on a Tree-house rental we owned at Carolina Trace in Sanford, North Carolina. I decided on a side trip to Roxboro, NC, Slaughter's home. I was directed by an Afro-American gas station attendant to Slaughter's house. I drove down an unpaved hill between two large ponds and by a pickup truck, then up an unpaved driveway to a brick ranch house. It was nondescript to say the most, and hanging on the front door was a Christmas wreath with price tag still attached (This was August, 1987.) There was also a vine-covered trailer nearby and another one toward the rear. No one answered my knock but I heard a bellowing 'YAWP!' from down by the ponds. 'N'won thar, mon. Down hyar!'

"I drove down, introduced myself to a stocky fellow wearing a railroader's striped jacket, rubber boots, a goodoldboy's ball cap, tinted glasses and a bulky tobacco chew in his cheek, and told him I had seen him for the first time, playing the Phillies in 1946, when he short-hopped a sinking liner as it spun into foul territory and did a pop-up slide and in one motion burned a runner trying to go from first to third. All he could say, looking at my license plate was: 'Noo Yawk! Cum ta see me.' I asked how he felt and he said not bad, but 'ma foot's bin gaivin may sum trouble eva since I fouled off a pitch on it when ah wuz waith tha Yankees.' Ever the hero-worshiping fan, I said, 'That's a small price to pay for the career you had.'

"Now gimlet-eyed, he commented, 'It's *ma* goddamned foot!' Again I shook hands, and asked if he might sign an autograph on a sheet of tablet paper. He spat some tobacco, grinned a bit, and said 'Sure!' My Enos moment was over and I was gone. Now his commissioned painting hangs in my family room and will probably be donated to his museum collection in Roxboro along with this vignette some day."

Now what goes around comes around, especially if it is that cursed Country Slaughter coming around to score the winning run while

Johnny Pesky held onto the relay throw. That was during my first year as a Red Sox fan, and the incident kind of told me what being a fan was going to be like. But when I started writing away for autographs, Enos Slaughter was the only player who ever did this: he sent me a handwritten letter explaining that the Cards were on the road and that he would send me an autographed picture when they got back to St Louis – and he did.

So Jack and I both got his autograph. We have each other's, too.

ERRORS

My wife Jean likes a lot of things about baseball, but she enjoys errors more than anything else. She particularly likes them if they are committed by the other team, especially if they are committed by Derek Jeter. Her favourite play in baseball is the one that includes two or more errors. She laughs delightedly. One time in Sancti Spiritus, we saw a game in which Camagüey was using their great outfielder Leslie Anderson as a first baseman, and Anderson missed easy pop fouls from two Sancti Spiritus batters in a row. Jean became an instant Leslie Anderson fan, and enjoyed watching him sort of play first in the second World Baseball Classic.

I myself am not a fan of errors. I will accept an error by Derek Jeter that allows us Red Sox to score the tying run, but in general I like a game in which either team gets six hits and no errors. When I was the official scorekeeper for the Oliver Baseball Club, I was, as they say, "tough on the hitters." That is, when Ritchie Schneider's ground ball went between the Kelowna third baseman's legs, I gave the latter an error rather than Schneider a hit. They would both cry about it and call me names. Call me fair and square, I would say.

But I have always agreed with the cliché accredited to veteran managers – I can forgive physical errors before I can forgive mental errors. When it comes to young millionaires playing in major league stadiums, I am utterly unforgiving. If you are getting paid to play the game I love, you ought to know which base to throw to or how many are out.

Playing in the raggedy Twilight League of sandlot softball (no, not that hideous thing called Slo-Pitch), I took pride in knowing what to do, and cursed when my center fielder thought he should go for the runner crossing the plate instead of throwing to second to keep the guy who just drove in that run from going to second. Oh, man, I am still pissed off! As for the offensive half of the game: I invented a new stat for our team and league – the ABR. If you got caught in a rundown between third and home with one man out, you got an ABR written after your name in the scorebook. It stood for asshole base running.

As an infielder with a weak arm, I had to learn how to get the ball out of my glove quickly, and I knew ahead of time where to throw the ball, and I always knew the percentages. I hated it when I muffed a ground ball. But at least I wasn't one of those young bozos who were blessed with natural athletic ability but didn't love the game enough to know why you should hit the cutoff man.

ETTINGER

What a name: Jennifer Ettinger! When she was a little girl in Nova Scotia, she must have skipped along the road while reciting her name out loud. Wouldn't you? Her father Ab Ettinger the amateur pitcher probably heard her as she skipped along. Heck, I feel like skipping when I hear the words Nova Scotia.

Jennifer Ettinger is an artist in Vancouver, and if you have gone to a ball game at Nat Bailey Stadium in the past year or so, you have seen some of her work. On the stadium facade there are huge enlarged prints of some of her portraits of famous dead ball players. Inside the concourse is her colourful sculpture/painting of Bob Brown Bear, an ursine rendition of a storied Vancouver baseball pioneer, player, manager, owner, who brought baseball to Vancouver and kept it here. One year the city of Vancouver invited artists to create their versions of Spirit Bears, and Ettinger's is so popular that this year they let her do two sculpture/paintings on this year's theme, an eagle in flight.

As an aside, I would like to say that I am attracted to Ettinger's work, because she takes as subjects three of the four essentials of human life. She does baseball, jazz and poetry. She omits only Mexican food. She doesn't even *eat* Mexican food, even when there's a Mexican restaurant in the neighbourhood. She did a picture of Honus Wagner looking quietly ready to employ his club. She did Grover Washington Jr. holding his saxophone in front of a yellow shirt. Poetry? Listen up.

You've got to be good to get a contract to do one of these emblems for the city. I've never heard of anyone getting to do two in one year. One of Ettinger's eagles is a giant red and white Gordie Howe, who was apparently some kind of ice hockey player way back when. Well, Ettinger's husband Max was born and brought up in Saskatchewan, and so was this Mr Howe. There's probably a connection there.

But the other eagle is called Word Bird, and he is a new edition of a booklength poem entitled *Baseball,* which I first published a few years back. I was fortunate enough to have seen this guy in production, and I have to say that he is going to be worth standing and looking at for a while. This is true partly because if you look carefully you can see that he is wearing my glasses, my Vancouver Canadians cap, my lapis lazuli ring and my orange low-cut Chuck Taylor All-Stars. But more important that that, the verses from the aforementioned poem are written all over his back.

At the faint risk of seeming immodest, I have to say that I love this bird. When I was a little boy I dreamed often that I could fly, but when I grew up I thought that I might be able to find out what poetry has to do with the equally important art of baseball.

EXTRA

When you are sitting in the stands in late September, and it is getting colder as midnight approaches, and they have changed pitchers eight times, and the game is already three and a half hours old, and you are, after all, watching the Orioles and the Royals, both teams twenty games out, and the game goes into extra innings, what are you supposed to say?

"Oh, boy! Free baseball!"

One Sunday in late August of 1968 in Montreal, I dropped in at Artie and Mary's place (Well, it was really Mary's place. You know Artie). No one was home, but the door was unlocked despite the collection of wonderful stuff in there, so I decided to go in and wait for someone to come home. I turned on the television set and started to watch the Red Sox game while I was waiting.

When I sat down we were in the fifth inning at Memorial Stadium in Baltimore, and Gary Bell was not very sharp, but he had a 2–0 lead, so I thought I would take in maybe an inning or two, and if no one came home I'd leave a note and take off home. In the seventh inning Bell got into trouble, so Sparky Lyle came in to help. In the eighth Lyle got into trouble, so Lee Stange came in to help. But by the end of the eighth inning the score was 2–2. Oh oh, I thought. It looks like extra innings. But come on, these were my Red Sox, and though they were not going to repeat as American League champions, they were still a couple games ahead of the Yankees, and that was reason enough to sit still and watch.

But I had to watch the last couple hours without a cigarette. I didn't want to phone home, because I didn't think I would be able to win the argument that might start. And besides, most extra inning games are decided in the tenth or eleventh, aren't' they? Pretty soon I began to hope that Artie or Mary didn't come home, so I could watch in peace. Okay, not peace. I was jumpy for five reasons. But if you have invested three hours in a baseball game, you can't just up and skedaddle. If you did, someone would hit a home run five minutes after you closed the door.

You can guess (or remember) what happened. In the bottom of the 18th inning, Jerry Stephenson, Boston's sixth and least accurate pitcher, gave up a wild pitch and double by Boog Powell, and the Orioles' third run came home. Artie did not.

So I was sad and irritable from nicotine deprivation, and I felt guilty for wasting my Sunday when I could have been working on whatever book I was working on. But I had acquired a memory that left a mark from 1968 that did not include police batons or flying cobblestones. I consider myself a "real" baseball fan because I like long low-scoring games.

Of course I like them better when my team wins, as when on March 10, 2009, the Netherlands beat the all-star Dominican Republic 2–1 in the eleventh inning, to knock the favourites out of the second World Baseball Classic tournament. I pranced in front of my easy chair and laughed out loud – in Dutch.

FAIN

The other morning, while thinking of the title for this piece, I reflected on the fact that you don't see that name Ferris often. Then I left the bathroom and looked at the newspaper in the dining room. In a minute or two I saw a reference to John Hughes ("Ferris Bueller's Day Off"). This stuff happens all the time, and lets you know that no matter how you try to order things you are paying attention to, those things are spending time ordering you around.

I will give an example. Back when I was in my mid-adolescence I was gaga about baseball, and in particular about baseball players' names. So I would make up fantasy teams determined by something interesting in the team-members' names.

You have to understand that this is a subject separate from the dice game baseball league I made up, the one in which the St Louis Browns won the World Series two years in a row. I will, as I said, give you an example. It started with Ferris Fain, a terrific first baseman who never had enough *cachet*, probably because (a) he did not hit home runs, and (b) he played for the Philadelphia Athletics. He won the American League batting championship in 1951, and again in 1952, when he also led the league in doubles and on-base percentage. Where did he land in the MVP voting? Sixth, both years.

But he had an alliterative name, and with him as an example I set out to fashion a lineup of alliterative major leaguers for the mid-century:

Catcher: Wes Westrum · Giants
First base: Ferris Fain · Athletics
Second base: Sibby Sisti · Braves
Third base: Ken Keltner · Indians
Shortstop: Marty Marian · Cardinals
Left field: Wally Westlake · Pirates
Center field: Dom DiMaggio · Red Sox
Right field: Jackie Jensen · Senators
Starting pitcher: Robin Roberts · Phillies
Relief pitcher: Dick Donovan · Braves
Batboy: Garth Garreau · Giants
Pinch hitter: Snuffy Sternweiss · Yankees
Pinch hitter: Mickey Mantle · Yankees
Manager: Red Rolfe · Tigers

You could complain about Dick Donovan as not truly alliterative, but I would argue that no one ever called him Richard. As for Sternweiss and Mantle as bench riders? Well, look, they were Yankees.

FAN

You have probably seen this guy. He's sitting by himself in the stands wearing a really old Mets cap, a scorebook on his lap and no popcorn anywhere near him. Usually he's a kind of old guy, but last summer I was glad to see a young guy, maybe twenty-three doing this. He might have his own system for recording stuff, but I'll bet he writes 7 and not F7 for a fly caught by the left fielder in fair territory.

This guy is a baseball fan. I have seen him and met him all over the place. I have seen him sport his entire well-worn Mets stuff to a game in Washington because he was in an exile called retirement. His baseball fan wise guy talk in the stands came down the row in a New York accent. I often see him at Nat Bailey Stadium. He sits in the same seat every game, with his oxygen tank in a little cart only a step away.

I will tell you who is not a fan. I refer to this guy as an attendee. He is sitting in the front row with his kids beside him. They are wearing new baseball caps, new baseball shirts and new baseball wristbands, and they are carrying huge clouds of cotton candy, jugs of Pepsi, new baseballs, and video game players. I'll tell you what this guy does in his front row: when a fair ball skips into foul territory and the runner is rounding first, this guy reaches down and tries to grab the ball. He wants to grab it and hold it high and arouse the cheers of the people around him, including his two kids.

Here's another things this guy does, and he is joined by hundreds of attendees all over the park: when a hitter for the visiting team hits a sacrifice fly to bat in the go-ahead run in the top of the ninth, he cheers like crazy because the right fielder caught the ball for the first out. Here's another thing this guy and his pals do: when the opposing pitcher throws over to first three times, he boos. A chorus of boos goes up, and I wonder to myself and my neighbours – what are all these hockey fans doing here?

Of course, if the same pitcher fakes a throw to second, this non-fan and his associates will start yelling "Balk!" or more likely, "Bock!"

These guys hate 1–0 games. If one of the starting pitchers has a no-hitter going in the sixth, they probably don't know it.

The baseball fan knows, though. He probably knows the pitcher's WHIP, and how many left-handed hitters are coming up in the seventh. I would not be surprised to learn that in his bag he has a book to read on the bus ride home.

FIELDING

You might have guessed that this chapter was going to be about defensive play, especially since there was an earlier one called "Errors." But no, it is about my favourite writer about baseball. I didn't say "baseball writer," because to me that denotes a sports reporter who specializes in the great game. No, I mean that among the literary types I like to read there are several who write poems and fiction about baseball sometimes, and among them – Joel Oppenheimer, Jack Spicer, Jerome Charyn, for examples – my favourite is Fielding Dawson, Fee, as he was called by his friends in the bars and magazines.

Dawson came from Missouri and grew into the literary life in New York City. If you asked me why I like his style better than that of others, I would only be able to say that I would rather watch Ted Williams's swing than Yogi Berra's. They both won MVP awards, and Yogi got to play in the World Series a lot, but I would rather go back in time and watch Ted Williams fly out to the warning track than see Yogi Berra hit a ball that was out of the strike zone out of the park. If you don't know what I mean, as Louis Armstrong might have said about these sluggers, there is no explaining it.

Maybe it would make sense if I said that Fielding Dawson is the kind of player who makes a tough play look easy as pie. You love the way people in his stories talk, including the narrator. They remind you that people don't really talk the way they usually do in books.

And he delights in little things that most people will not remember or even notice. In his book about Black Mountain, the experimental college headed those years by Charles Olson:

While I was in the Army John and Elaine Chamberlain were there, and John warmly tells the story, now, of Elaine in right field picking flowers, while Jonathan Williams was at bat, and five times in a row Jonathan hit high drives to right field, and five times in a row, she glanced up, saw the ball in the air, left her flowers, and caught it.

Aw, what can I say that will convey this singular writer's gift and practice? I can only urge you to find and read his stories, look for them, because he was not published by those New York Doubledays and all that. Find *A Great Day for a Ball Game* and read it in one sitting as I did. It's a love story set in the big city by a guy who pitches for a softball team in Central Park. The quotation from Ernie Banks makes a great title that is both innocent and ironic.

Better yet, try to find my favourite baseball book of all time, seventy-page *The Greatest Story Ever Told*. It too is about baseball and love, but in this case it is teenage love. And, I guess I should add, teenage sex. Well, every good fiction presents something you didn't know anything about.

FIRST

If you are going to play first base you should be a big person who hits for power and maybe doesn't move very fast or very far. It helps if you have a name like Walt (Dropo) or Harmon (Killebrew) or Luke (Easter). Any manager likes to have a first baseman who can field the ball the way Andreas Galarraga did, but if the truth be told a lot of sluggers have been "hidden" at first, and a lot of old outfielders have been moved to first to get a few more years out of their bats, even now that the American League has the DH for that purpose.

I moved to first base for my last few years in the Twilight League. I had been an infielder all my life, and never all that fast at any position, but I think that I was persuaded to move to first base to minimize my hospital visits. This was in my sixties, you have to understand. I still had pretty good reflexes, but not on every play.

During the heady days of the Kosmik League in Vancouver, meaning the early seventies about the time that I was in my late thirties, I played shortstop for the Granville Grange Zephyrs, a bunch of painters and poets. I was named the all-star shortstop two years in a row, partly because the team was chosen by the sports staff of the *Georgia Straight* alternative newspaper, and I was that staff. I threw to first on an arc, but made up for my lack of arm by the dazzling speed with which I got the ball out of my short-fingered glove.

In my forties and early fifties I switched to second base, still my favourite position because of the neat way you turn to finish the double play. There I got a one-hopper in the eye and had my wrist broken by a runner who did not slide, but my reflexes were still pretty good. But my range was going, so in my late fifties and into my sixties I played third base. There it was that I discovered that my reflexes were not of premier quality. I got a line drive in the other eye.

So for the rest of my playing days I moved to first base. It was fun digging throws out of the dirt and leaping high to snare wild ones. I gave up my old shortstop nickname, Whip, and went by my lady friend's moniker for me, Bubba. I will admit that finishing a double play is not as much fun as starting one, and definitely not as much fun as making the relay to first, but it is still better than sitting here in retirement, writing about it.

And I did not retire at age sixty-eight because of any diminution of my glove work. I retired because I had broken my hip in a fall while being attacked by a dog with grey eyes, and I could not run the bases any more. And yes, I do remember the rejoinder made by my lady friend when I first made that announcement.

FURILLO

Alliteration was not the only thing I liked about ballplayers' names, though it was the main reason I liked Robin Roberts better than the Phils' other terrific starter Curt Simmons. There was also the failed experiment I started with the example of Carl Furillo.

I really liked Furillo. I liked everybody on those wonderful Brooklyn teams, and my only sense of New York came from baseball magazines, movie musicals and the verses of Damon Runyan. Furillo led the National League in hitting one year, but his nickname was "The Rifle," referring to the power and accuracy of his throws from right field, and the respect with which an opposing baserunner stayed close to the bag he was lucky enough to have attained.

Right fielder Carl "The Rifle" Furillo. I sort of thought, being fifteen and not much of a linguist, that the name might have something to do with fury. But mainly I loved to say it and hear it, how all those words sound as if they were meant to go together. I know that he got the nickname because sportswriters do love alliteration, and he played as a young man for Reading. But there is no eff and there is no ell in Reading, so I preferred Carl "The Rifle" Furillo, right field.

Sports writers like to dish out nicknames, and sometimes they take the easy way out with ballplayers' names, coming up a few decades later with stuff like Goose Gossage or Moose Mussina. Phooey on that. I wanted, when I was fifteen, a name that used enough of the right letters and also meant something as specific as the rifle hanging off Carl Furillo's right shoulder.

I think that the first one I tried was George "The Elk" Kell. No, it does not roll off the tongue, and it is not a great description of the great third sacker. Jim "The Spiral" Piersall – now, that was pretty clever, but I remember that at the time I wished that the sportswriters would pay more attention to Jimmy's matchless defensive play and less to his nuttiness. How, I asked myself, about Joe "The Garage" Garagiola? A little obvious, sure, but didn't it suggest his willingness to get down and dirty behind the plate?

I was probably trying to get two of my interests together when I turned three ballplayers into poets. Bob "The Verse" Cerv, Hoot "The Verse" Evers, and Roy "The Verses" Sievers. You could add pitcher Howie "The Poet" Pollet. I think you begin to figure out why I referred to this fooling around as a "failed" experiment.

Still, if I was not a heavy thinker in those days, Ed Lopat was no Plato, Johnny Pesky was only a speck, and Ted Kluszewski? Maybe I could run away after I gave him his new nickname.

GARDENER

When I was spending my summers in Mexico City way back then, I used to read my baseball news in one of the big broadsheets, *El Universal* or more likely *Excelsior*. In the third paragraph, Tony Conigliaro of the Red Sox might be referred to as a *jardinero*. Luckily for me, I knew enough Spanish to know that *jardinero* means gardener, and luckily I was familiar enough with mid-century sports writing to know that gardener means outfielder. Calling an outfielder a gardener is an example of employing what is called, I think, the "elegant substitute."

    I did a lot of elegant substituting when I was a teenage baseball reporter for the Oliver *Chronicle* and later the Penticton *Herald*. How did I learn my baseball lingo? When I was a teenager I read *Sport, Sport Life, Baseball, Baseball Digest, Inside Sports,* and whatever other publications showed up at Frank's pool hall magazine rack. [You should know that just now I went back and deleted "magazines" and replaced it with "publications" because I didn't want to say "magazine" twice in a row. That is a low-grade elegant substitution.]

    Some of them were easy. The plate becomes the dish the second time around. The pitcher becomes a moundsman, and if he is a left-hander he turns into a portsider. I have to say that though I would be a little embarrassed by doing this sort of thing now, unless I could contact my inner irony, I loved hauling them out when I was a teenage reporter.

I think that the elegant substitute is or was related to the nickname. In your second paragraph you could call Ted Williams "the brooding US Marine Corps veteran," or you could just borrow "the Splendid Splinter." You could call the American League "that outfit stupid enough to keep the Designated Hitter after the three-year trial run," or just use the usual "junior circuit."

Sports writers gave elegant substitute names to all the major league teams. So in Chicago we had the Pale Hose, in Brooklyn the Bums, and in St Louis the Redbirds. In more recent times the imagination seems to have sagged, to that the Mariners are called the M's, the Orioles are called the O's, and the Rockies are called the Rocks. Come on! Do you prefer the "Yanks" to the "Bronx Bombers"? Would you refer to the Tribe as the I's?

When I was a teenage reporter I was disappointed when the local front office changed the Oliver team's name from the Elks to the OBC, and sewed those three letters on their shirts. It stood for Oliver Baseball Club, as colorless and unknowledgeable a moniker as you could fancy. I had to be satisfied with referring to them as "the locals" or "the home squad." Things got even worse when other teams in the league dropped their traditional nicknames and took on the names of their beer-company sponsors. One grew tired of calling the Labatts the "Suds."

But no elegant substitutes are as much fun as the long list of alternatives to a home run. Your subject might have just pounded out a four-bagger. Maybe a circuit blow. I once read "four-master," from some seashore reporter. Ball players have called them dingers and taters. In recent times the TV announcers have taken to referring to a "long fly." He went yard. A fence-clearing blast. A bases-clearing drive. A distant poke. Everyone's favourite? A Ruthian clout!

You can't get more elegant than that.

GEORGE

I was not crazy about my name when I was young. I even planned to change it to Theodore, so that I could be Ted, like you-know-who. Lately I have come to accept it, though I have gone by other cognomens, such as GB, Whip and Bubba. George means farmer, with the geo- connected to the earth, I guess. Maybe I should have been a groundskeeper. Or maybe I should have tried to cover more ground at short.

I should have concentrated more on playing second base. There has never been a hall-of-famer who played second and bore the name George. We have done all right at all other positions, but I should have worked harder and gone to Cooperstown as George "Whip" Bowering.

Otherwise, we could put together a pretty fair all-star team. Third base is easy, or is it a problem? Do we go for George Kell or George Brett? Kell's lifetime batting average was .306, and Brett's was .305, but Brett's power numbers were higher. I liked Kell better, but I'd settle for either and keep the other as my first pinch hitter.

On the other infield corner there can be no other choice than George Sisler. Only thirteen players ended with higher lifetime batting averages, and it took Joe DiMaggio and Ichiro Suzuki to beat the Major League records he had put up. At shortstop it's George Davis. Are you familiar with George Davis? Well, he was the first shortstop ever to lead his league in RBIs. He was a switch hitter who hit .373 one year, still a record. His achievements were better than the majority of shortstops in the hall of fame, but he did not get in till 1998, a century after his best season. He was treated worse by his wife. The day after he died of syphilis in a mental hospital she buried him in a cheap box in an unmarked grave.

Here's my catcher: Jorge Posada. At moments such as this I can put my Yankeephobia aside. Of course I'll do it again when it comes to my outfield – the enjoyable George Bell, who put in nine dandy years with the Blue Jays, but went elsewhere just before they won their world series rings, George Foster, who hit 52 homers in 1977, the pre-injection era, and of course the Bambino, George Herman Ruth Jr., from Baltimore.

For my manager I am going to take George "Sparky" Anderson, the first field boss, as they say, to manage a team from either league to a world series win. And here is how I am going to solve my second-base problem: Sparky is also playing second for me. Okay, he played one season as the regular second baseman of the Phillies, and batted .218. I will bat him eighth. But not ninth: my pitcher the legendary George Bamberger never got a hit in the majors.

Now I am insisting on a utility player, maybe the best of all time. I mean George van Haltren. In seventeen seasons with the Cubs, Brooklyn, Baltimore, Pittsburgh and the Giants, he pitched and played every position but catcher, while racking up an OPS of .802 and a win-loss record of 40–31. Despite having nearly a thousand more hits than does Johnny Evers, unlike the latter, he is not in the hall of fame.

He's on my team, though, by George!

GERMANS

At their home opener against the Angels in 2009 the Seattle Mariners fielded a lineup in which eight of the ten players bore Latin American names. The exceptions were designated hitter Ken Griffey Jr. and catcher Kenji Johjima. I have seen Caribbean lineups with fewer Latin names. Somewhere recently I read that in the big leagues today more than a third of the names are Spanish, and in the minors the percentage is higher. It appears that only the influx of Asian players will moderate the Spanification of the US American "national game."

There weren't many Spanish names in the majors when I was a kid. In the first half of the twentieth century and then some ballplayers tended to have German names. What was a patriotic baseball fan kid supposed to do? The Germans were the bad guys. We were glad when Joe Louis knocked off Max Schmeling, though it happened when we were babies in our English-Canadian mothers' arms. We were glad when Montgomery drove Rommell out of Africa. How could we cheer for Red Schoendienst and Warren Spahn? I guess that most of the time we didn't notice the German names. I wonder whether this was true for my pals Gordon Bauer and Rudy Knippelberg.

Actually there weren't as many German names in baseball at midcentury as there were a few decades earlier. As a baseball fan and a reader, I was pretty familiar with the history of the game. When I read the names Honus Wagner, Lou Gehrig, Charlie Gehringer, Frankie Frisch, Henry Heilmann, Edd Roush and so on, I wondered why it was that German-American boys took to baseball so easily? There wasn't any baseball in Germany, as far as I knew.

In the 1936 Olympics held in Berlin, baseball was a demonstration sport. Two teams made up of Americans played in front of a crowd of 90,000 people in Hitler's awesome stadium. The World Champions defeated the US Olympics 6–5. The losers had a pitcher named Heringer and the winners had a left fielder named Goldberg. I guess the latter is a kind of German name. I wonder which side Hitler and Himmler cheered for.

If we went back and checked the rosters carefully, we would probably find out that there were as many Irish-Americans as German-Americans in professional baseball from 1875 to 1950. But could they field an all-star team to face these guys?

C Ray Schalk
1B Lou Gehrig
2B Charlie Gehringer
3B Mike Schmidt (all right, he is a time traveller)
SS Honus Wagner
LF Heinie Manush
CF Harry Heilmann

RF Chuck Klein
RHP Red Ruffing
LHP Eddie Plank
MGR Casey Stengel

GREEN

There is a photograph that my sweetheart took of me standing in Fenway Park about an hour before game time. I don't know whether I have seen so much green in one place in my entire life, unless you count the Washington Nationals pitching rotation. It's too bad the Red Sox don't wear the Oakland Athletics' colours, but then they would not be wearing red socks. They would be as goofy as the Chicago White Sox, who wear something that looks like black sox. A few decades ago, when the White Sox were trimmed in red, they wore red socks with little images of white socks on them. [By the way, the Everett AquaSox wear black sox to go with their aqua caps.]

It doesn't matter – green is baseball's colour. In the middle of our grey hazy cities there used to be walled-in gardens of green called something such as Wrigley Park or Three Rivers Stadium. Nowadays they are named after insurance companies and dog food, but they are still verdant areas where parents can take their children to enjoy a respite from the surrounding concrete and plastic – except in Toronto and St. Petersburg. So it was in the nineteenth century, when US industry was putting up smoke-puking chimneys in any city of size. Baseball came along and offered a reminder of pre-industrial America, of Eden, even. In June of 1846, several years after games played in Upper Canada, "the first baseball game with set rules" was played in Hoboken, New Jersey, at a place called Elysian Field. You will remember that the original Elysian Fields were reserved as a resting place for great heroes who were now dead – sort of like the Polo Grounds for the 1962 Mets.

When Vida Blue pitched for the Athletics he wore his name in green on his back. I sometimes wear my initials on a baseball cap styled for the Double-A Greenville Braves. Unfortunately the colours are Atlanta Braves colours, and they have been moved to Mississippi, anyway. [The only good thing about that is getting to type Mississippi – twice.] I wish I had been able to watch the Bowling Green Barons, but they played in the Kitty League when I was a tot.

There have been a lot of major league players named Green, starting with Ed Green, who was born in Philadelphia in 1850, and pitched one year for the brand new Philadelphia Athletics in 1890. He was forty years old, and had a 7–15 season for a team that finished eighth in the American Association. He made history by giving up a grand slam homer and a three-run homer in the same game to Ed Cartwright of the St. Louis Browns. It was the first time such a feat had been accomplished. Nowadays we have one Kahlil Greene, a shortstop who is blond despite his name, and is currently hitting .234 for the Cardinals. Like Ed Green, he was born in Pennsylvania, a state in which the future Oakland Athletics wore blue.

But my favourite was Jim Greengrass, a perfect name for baseball, as far as I am concerned. When I was a kid he played for the Reds (hmm) and (you guessed it) Philadelphia. He did not amount to much after a dandy first couple years, but what a name! I liked it so much that I published lots of poems and book reviews as E.E. Greengrass.

GREYBEARD

"Wait till next year!" What a wonderful cry! When I was a kid that was what the Brooklyn Dodgers fans shouted in September. The end of the season just meant you had to make do with inferior sports until April, when you got to hope again. We especially loved the Dodgers because they kept promising to be good and win a World Series for the first time after decades of failure. "Next year" was a package of hope and irony – sometimes you were glad about their perfect record for failure, because it gave you something to look forward to. Ironically.

They lost in 1916, 1920, 1941, 1947, 1949, 1952, and 1953. When I was a kid they were in the World Series most years, and lost to the Yankees every time. "Wait till next year," I shouted the October when I was thirteen, a demonic smile all over my face. Then in 1955 they beat the Yankees and won it all, and then the Brooklyn Dodgers folded their arms and quit trying.

Playing poetic guerrilla softball for decade after decade, I could hardly, when the rains of winter started, wait till next year. You know how they say that teenagers think they will live forever? When you are a talented but not highly talented softball player, you sort of think that you will play ball all your life. When a hard ground ball goes wham into your glove and you skip once and peg it to first, you are by these actions stepping out of the constraints of time and space. You have the kind of perfect health they hand out to all the people newly arrived in Heaven.

Then a short-hop breaks your occipital bone and you are out for the last month of the season. A few years later a line drive that you never see comes off the bat fifty feet away and blinds you for a while. You lie there listening to a youngster call the ambulance. "I don't know," he says, "thirty something, I guess." Your first baseperson snorts. You are in your early sixties. This kind of occurrence starts you thinking that someday soon there might not be a next year. You might die, as your earlier first baseman did, or you might break your hip and put an end to your putative running days.

Being a greybeard, I have a particular interest in greybeards. I am notorious for staffing my fantasy team the High Sox with older players. As of this writing I have Jamie Moyer in my rotation. When I was a lad I adored Satchell Paige and Connie Marrero, two pitchers who were American League rookies after long careers as superstars in the Negro Leagues and the Cuban leagues. I am glad to have been a baseball fan over the decades when Minnie Miñoso made his major league plate appearances, from April 19, 1949 to October 5, 1980. In 2003 he drew a walk in his only appearance for the St. Paul Saints. He was either 77 or 80, depending on which Cuban source you are sourcing. Oh, and his US career would have begun up to a decade earlier if he had not had the problems of being black and Cuban.

Then there is my friend Lionel Kearns the poet and amateur hockey player. He has a pure white beard, and he skates in an over-70 league. In a couple of years he hopes to be rookie of the year in an over-75 league he knows about. He doesn't have to wait till next year. Those old coots play all year round.

HATS

Really, I think that you should call them caps, but I have done my five C's, and so we will call them hats. Baseball hats. I have collected various things in my life: frog figurines, books by Jerome Charyn (including *The Seventh Babe*, my favourite baseball novel), university teeshirts, and baseball hats. I started my teeshirt collection with a University of California at Santa Barbara teeshirt, and I started my baseball hat collection with a Baltimore Orioles hat, the one with the cartoon oriole on the front. It is way too small for me.

In case you are thinking of adding to my collection, I wear a size 8. Sometimes I can squeeze into a 7⅞. I have a lot of baseball hats, though I have restrictive rules. If I am going on a shortish trip, as when going to five parks in California, for example, I can acquire one hat. If we are driving clear across the continent, I can get two. For this reason, I had to pass up very attractive hats in Schaumberg and Amarillo. Sometimes I have to pass up wonderful hats, as with the Mazatlán Venados, because the shops don't stock anything bigger than a 7½. Pinheads are privileged.

I garnered my favourite hat at the last ballpark in a trip that passed through New England and the Maritimes. The ballpark was the Stade Municipal in Québec, and the hat is that worn by the Capitales of the CanAm League. It is navy blue with a golden capital Q, inside of which is a white baseball with red stitching and a navy blue *fleur de lis* in the middle of the baseball. It sounds kind of cluttered, and I prefer non-cluttered caps such as that worn by the Pittsburgh Pirates, but it looks really good.

Do I have to mention that for my collection of hats I insist on a fitted cap, unless that is entirely impossible? For example that Greenville Braves cap my sweetheart ordered just before they left town: there weren't any fitted caps left in the store, and this was the only way to get a hat with my initials on it. Okay, fan hats if necessary. But here is a trend I really detest (it is as bad as the decals the Pirates used to stick all over their batting helmets): those horrible pre-curled bills on fan hats. If you have a big head like mine you do not want a stupid narrow curled bill sticking out above your nose. I am no fan of hip-hop, but I understand their protest against curled baseball hat peaks. They leave the peaks dead flat and they don't take the manufacturer's stickers off.

Well, the baseball cap has become the world's main headwear. If you go to Laos or Sicily or Ecuador, you'll see guys in sandals, teeshirts and baseball caps. If you go to restaurants in Canada now you will see uneducated louts sitting with their forearms on the table and their caps on their heads. It used to be that when an NHL player scored three goals in a game a lot of fedoras would be thrown onto the ice. Now it's likely to be ball caps made of plastic mesh. I once checked out ball caps on people in the streets in northern Europe. The most popular one was from a football team – the Washington Redskins. They are nuts about Red Indians in Europe.

Oh, and I hope that you have guessed by now – I don't wear my baseball hat backward. That used to be done by hip Black kids in the forties. Now it is done by slack-jawed blond kids with white wires hanging from their ears.

HENRY

I visited my doctor today about things to do with blood pressure and neurology and unmentionables, and the first thing he said to me was, "Where do you get ideas for your books?" Now this is a question that non-writers often put to writers, but for me on this one occasion it was interesting, because I was looking for an idea for this very book we are reading. I had finished one of the five H chapters and was wondering what I would start on next.

It happens that my doctor's name is Henry Chong. If you are like me, you grew up surrounded by a popular so-called culture that usually portrayed a person named Henry in a comic vein. Take Henry Aldridge, for example, and all you young people can look him up but that wont help much. Or the comic strip "Henry," about a little bald-headed kid who never said anything. Oh Henry! chocolate bars weren't all that comical but Henry Higgins was.

So when Henry Aaron took over from Willie Mays as the big threat to Babe Ruth's lifetime home run record, the sports writers tried to evade the name Henry and retool the man as "Hammerin' Hank." But was he really a Hank? The last great Hank had been Hank Greenberg, and no one ever referred to him as Henry. They called him "Hammerin'" too. Greenberg was the first Jewish superstar in baseball (though I don't remember hearing the term "superstar" until late in the century). and Henry Aaron was one of the first African-American superstars (though I don't remember hearing the term "African American" until after he had beaten Ruth's mark). The only other Hank I recall right now is Hank Thompson. He integrated the St. Louis Browns in 1947, but he had to wear the same name as some country singer who was famous for drinkin' songs. The latter might have been known as "Hammered Hank."

If you look around carefully, you'll find some pretty interesting Henrys in baseball history. Henry Chadwick was a nineteenth-century cricket reporter who came over to baseball and invented statistics, thus presenting the game with one of its greatest delights. Heinie Manush's real name was Henry. He was a great hitter and the first guy to get thrown out of a World Series game for snapping the elastic bow tie of an umpire. John Henry "Pop" Lloyd was the greatest shortstop in the Negro Leagues. And my childhood hero Peewee Reese? His middle name was Henry.

Still, you can see why players and others went for nicknames if their parents called them Henry. Remember "Dance with me, Henry"? It was a corny song sung by a lot of corny singers in the fifties, and it was also the title of one of the worst Abbot and Costello movies and the last they ever made.

By the way, I never call my doctor "Hammerin' Hank." And I hope he doesn't get his doctoring ideas from me.

HIGH

My fantasy ball team, despite my having drafted in genius fashion, is at the time of this writing in fourth place in my five-team division, ninth out of ten overall. I don't have to tell you that my ill fortune is due to injuries and inexplicable slumps on the parts of my all-star catcher and shortstop. This is my fourteenth season at the helm of the currently disappointing High Sox.

Most of the other owners in my league change the names of their teams as the fancy takes them, but I am a conservative when it comes to baseball. No Vancouver High Sox of Anaheim for me! And definitely no Hi Sox.

I have some friends in the baseball fan world who do not look kindly on my having a fantasy team. They think of it as somehow demeaning to the game or the fandom the game requires. As a purist, I may have felt that way in the past – i.e. before I got a team. I will admit that having a team changes the way one scans the box scores in the morning. Of course I look and see how the Red Sox managed to lose once again, but I will admit that I check out my Pujols and my Rollins. As for watching games on television? I like it best when the Red Sox are on, though I own a National League team, but I also face certain quandaries: when my Haren is pitching against my Ethier, do I hope that the latter hits a triple and is stranded on third?

Here's another problem. I named the team the High Sox because that is the way I like players to be attired (I mean even that twit A-Rod wears them high). But I did not select my roster according to the height of the hosiery. Well, I say, it is a fantasy team, all right? In my fantasy Geovany Soto wears stirrups that come up to his knees. He also reads the poetry of Robin Blaser in the clubhouse. Or he reads the work of Miguel Batista, a poet I was proud to have in my rotation in the early part of the century.

Even though he wore his trousers down to his spikes.

HOME

George Carlin, in a famous routine about the differences between football and baseball, said, "Baseball begins in the spring, the season of new life. Football begins in the fall, when everything's dying." All right! He also said about the aim of the players that in football one uses all kinds of military manoeuvres to invade the enemy's zone, whereas in baseball one wants to get home, to be safe at home.

In this sense, you might say that baseball is a classic game. If you go to the most famous epic of all time, the *Odyssey*, you will find that the main desire of its hero Odysseus is to get home. Monsters and horny women try to stop him but nothing can make him stray from his intention to reach home, in his home park in Ithaca.

Presiding at home, in the case of the *Odyssey*, is Penelope, who spends her days at the loom. Presiding at home in our own story of heroes is the catcher, the guy with the best view in the park. It is a cliché to say that the catcher has the whole game in front of him, the only defensive player who does. He it is who starts each play by signalling his desire to the pitcher. All the other players see the pitcher from behind or in their peripheral vision. The catcher it is who sets into play the challenges that will come to these other players. He is the custodian of home and the foreman of the whole spread.

Before I was born, when my father was a baseball player, he played first base. I have his old box scores in a green metal box. He seemed to get his team's important hits, but they were usually singles. By the time that I got to watch him play (and if you have seen your father play ball you know how neat that is) the game was fastball, and he was a catcher. This despite the fact that he was missing most of the index finger on his throwing hand. I watched him carefully, though I did not seem to be doing so, and it was from him that I learned the little motions and angles that a catcher has.

My mother was a catcher too. I think that she became a catcher not because she was a homemaker but because she was vying against her blonde competition for his attention, he being her softball coach. When I was a kid in the first couple years of elementary school, I had no idea that it was an unusual privilege to see one's mother squatting with a metal mask over her face and a chest protector covering the front of her. You have no idea how much I wish that I could go back now and watch my mother behind the plate. The old baseball lingo denoting the catcher's gear is "the tools of ignorance." As a kid I knew that the catcher pretty well had to be the smartest guy on the team; that's why he is most likely to become a manager or a radio and television announcer. They were called the tools of ignorance for the same reason that people said tut tut when they looked at an old catcher's bent fingers. Why would you choose such a position, they are asking.

When I was around fourteen or fifteen I decided, because of my parentage, to play catcher for the British Columbia team at Air Cadet camp in Abbotsford. I found out why a person might choose that position the day I threw out two runners at second base. I don't know how I did it – I was not famous for the oomph in my arm. But going into my squat for the next pitch by our guy Smith from Kamloops, I felt like the smartest guy on the lot.

HOTDOG

The classic food menu for baseball consists of unshelled peanuts and hotdogs. No one ever eats Cracker Jack at a ball game. You could add beer, but that's not really food, is it? Or is it? The bun in a hotdog is made of wheat and beer is made of barley, so what's the difference? Back in the old days at the Cecil Pub, whenever anyone said we should eat something, one of us would say, "There's a sandwich in every glass!"

Speaking of beer at ball games, last fall in Baltimore I finally caved in and ordered a Bud, or maybe it was a Miller. I didn't order a Lite, because US beer is already light. This was the first time I had ever tried one of these things at a ballpark. I'm sorry, but I could not finish it. Having experienced a ballpark beer of some other name in Minnesota, I knew that I would be getting a beer-flavoured liquid. But it was so repulsive that I just stood the half-empty plastic bottle under my seat as far back as it would go.

But hotdogs, eh? They used to cost a quarter. Now I have not looked yet this year, but aren't they around twenty dollars each? I have said somewhere that the best hotdog I ever had was at a game in the drizzle on a hill above Basel, Switzerland. It was one of the worst games I have ever seen, played between two teams of Swiss guys coached by unknown US American guys. I think that one of the teams was called the Eagles. But I would stand in the drizzle and watch them play again if I could have one of those Swiss hotdogs.

Among the worst hotdogs I have had at a ballgame were the many Shopsy's dogs I forced down my throat at Jarry Park in Montreal during the first two years of the Expos. I would go to these games with my friend Ed Pechter, who was also the centerfielder for the York Street Tigers, my ball team. Ed would eat five Shopsy's dogs at each game, and he would put no condiments on them, just plain little wiener on white bread bun. I would like to say that the baseball playing was opposite to that in Basel as well, but these were the Expos of John Boccabella (lifetime .219) and Mack Jones (lifetime .252), the fans' favourites in 1969.

Of course the word "hotdog" has another meaning in baseball. "Put some mustard on that boy," players shout when they see some newbie showing off a certain way. I somehow learned the Panamanian expression for such behaviour, but I can't seem to find it in print. It sounds something like *postaista*. It worked when I shouted it at Manny Sanguillén, who was showboating while warming up an A's pitcher in the Kingdome. He turned his head fast and looked for me in the stands low along the right field foul line. I hope he was smiling inside; I liked Manny a lot. Who wouldn't?

INCHES

All those automatic remarks people make about baseball. It's ninety percent pitching. The game isn't over till the last man's out. Never make the first or third out at third base. It's a game of inches.

Bases loaded, that drive to right field was foul by inches. Put the tying run on with a slider that missed the outside corner by inches. One-hopper eluded the diving Barmes by inches.

An inch is one-twelfth of a foot. An ounce, which word comes from the same source, is a sixteenth of a pound. This ridiculous but nostalgically endearing system of measurements has been dumped everywhere except the USA and maybe two little countries somewhere in the mist, but wherever you go in baseball the ancient markers go too. It's a wonder baseball (and the USA) doesn't use cubits and furlongs.

"It's a game of centimeters," I like to proclaim when I sit in a US ballpark and witness a close play at first.

In the good old days the fences at the Big Owe in Montreal had numbers painted in them to show you how many meters you'd have to hit a fly ball to achieve a home run. "That was a 104.7 meter drive, Mel."

If, say, the United States enters the worldwide metric system in the twenty-second century, what will happen to the dimensions of the great summer game? I am thinking of the mule-headed anti-metric types who put signs inside elevators to inform us that the maximum weight for the car is 1179.3 kilograms.

We are always being reminded that Abner Doubleday was a genius for choosing the distance of 90 feet between bases and ensuring millions of close plays at first. Leaving aside the question of whether Abner was ever on a ball field, we can easily imagine that those bang-bang plays would happen if we made it 100 feet between bases, or even 90 meters. In softball it's sixty feet and no easier to steal second than it is in baseball.

If we went for metric baseball, would we have to remark on a home run by saying that Griffey went "meter" instead of yard? Maybe Barry Foote, the onetime catcher for the Expos and Yankees, would have to think of a name change.

Not going to happen. Fans of US games are going to have to get used to being thought of the way people think of those guys who dress up in medieval outfits and go out sword fighting on the heath. Anachronism just makes an activity or hobby more seductive. In a game in which the focus is on a ball wrapped in cowhide and called "the ole horsehide," every retreat from everyday life is welcome. Artificial turf came and went. There is hope that the batting glove will follow. We can laugh at the artificiality all we want. But remember: if you want to sit in a grandstand and watch the inane invasion of the real world, there's always NASCAR.

INDIANS

1948 was the greatest year in the history of human civilization, even though my dad's team, the Cleveland Indians, defeated my team, the Boston Red Sox, in that notorious playoff ruined by Lou Boudreau, a guy with an Acadian name. I knew the names of all the Indians, including Chief Wahoo, who was on their hat. Chief Wahoo was a comic character in a comic strip that kept changing its name as the main character disappeared. In those days it seemed as if everyone thought it was all right to name teams after the people the U S Americans had tried to wipe out.

I looked at my lovely baseball magazines, at the colour pictures of the various Cleveland Indians. I don't remember seeing any Indians. The famous Indian at the time was Allie Reynolds, but he had been traded by Cleveland to the Yankees after the 1946 season. There were two African Americans, this being the year after Jack Robinson made it to the majors. These were future Hall-of-Famers, Larry Doby and Satchell Paige. We called them Negroes in those days, just as we called First Nations peoples Indians. And there was a young guy named Al Rosen getting ready to take the third base position from Ken Keltner. I had no idea that Rosen was a Jewish name. In the South Okanagan Valley where I grew up we had lots of Indians but no Jews.

In the South Okanagan, which is just north of Washington State's Okanogan Valley, the Indians played a lot of baseball. They had a whole league, and I guess you might say that they were our version of the Negro Leagues. One of their teams was called the White Men. It was a lot of fun watching the Indians play ball. There was way more showboating than we got in the regular Okanagan Mainline Baseball League. And it was a little noisier. Remember all those images we used to be fed about the silent stoicism of the American Indian? It didn't happen in Indian baseball.

When the Wenatchee Chiefs, a team in the white Western International League, held their spring training in my hometown Oliver, our Chief Manuel Louie said the players could use his sweat lodge if they let him work out with them. Manuel Louie was an overweight fifty-something, and a bit bowlegged. But he could still snatch ground balls and make the throw to first. He looked like an Indian Honus Wagner.

INJURIES

Once in a playoff game, I think it was, Bobby Baun, the Toronto Maple Leafs defenceman, played the last period and a half with a broken leg. In hockey you often see a guy come back from the dressing room with a dozen stitches sewn into his face, ready to go out there for his next shift. I think that football players keep going with pretty bad wounds, and that rugby players and Australian Rules footies do too. Boxers often put up with broken hands. If you could believe your eyes you would assume that professional wrestlers keep going with deep lacerations in their chests and eyeballs.

Basketball stars, though, will sit in five-thousand dollar suits all the way through the playoffs rather than get back on that floor and possibly aggravate an injury that might endanger their career statistics. Well, basketball is a game in which you have to make quick starts and stops, and in which you might get someone's thumb in your eye. Delicate complicated machines, those seven-footers.

But look at baseball. The number two starter in your rotation might miss an appearance or two because he has a blood blister. Baseball is a game of exact spots. I was there when the great Edgar Martinez became the best designated hitter in the American League. Before the exhibition game in question he had been a third baseman. But he was playing a pre-season game under the dome in Vancouver, an arena that was not often used for baseball. I guess the comparatively inexperienced groundskeepers did not get the turf around first base laid precisely. Edgar caught his shoe while trying to steal second, and missed the beginning of the 1993 season with a torn hamstring.

If you hit the ball a quarter-inch off the sweet spot on the bat you get a harmless fly ball. If the ball takes a bad hop it can hit you in the face as it did when I got my cracked occipital bone. If you have your hand wrong when you are sliding into home you can snap a wrist. It's a game of tiny adjustments. A blister on a finger of your pitching hand can wreck your ERA and your team's chances to win a series.

If you are an offensive tackle in the NFL you can play all you want to with a blood blister on your finger or your nose. You don't have to locate a curve ball low on the outside corner of the plate. If you are a hockey forward with blood welling behind your right eye you can join the mad scramble in front of your opponents' net. You don't have to take the ball off the wall your shoulder has just crashed against and turn and hit the cutoff man two hundred feet away.

I once played the last four innings of a game with a broken left wrist. I even got a pop single my last time at bat. But it was just fun, not a do or die situation.

INTERLEAGUE

Every few years the non-fans of baseball bring in something to piss off the old-time fans. Often it will be something adapted from the practices in football or basketball or even hockey, for heaven's sake. Take for example interleague play. We should have known that this was coming when we let them get away with playoffs leading to the World Series. In hockey and basketball nearly all teams make the playoffs, and in Canadian football the season is used to eliminate a quarter of the teams. My sweetheart Jean and I have two suggestions for the National Hockey League. I say forget the regular season and just start in September with the playoffs. She says they should just eliminate the puck.

Here is one thing you know for sure about the playoffs and the fact that the suits keep adding more rounds: no matter how often the manipulators say that they are trying to please the fans in more cities, the reason for all these tasteless moves is to rake in more dollars. They try a similar phony argument regarding interleague play: fans will get to see the teams they have never been able to see. Har dee har. I live in Vancouver, along with a couple million other people, and if I want to see a major league baseball game, I have to hit the road. Maybe I can look forward to regular scheduled games to be brought to my city.

Wait a minute: they are already doing that. The Buffalo Bills play in Toronto. The San Francisco Giants play in Tokyo. The first NBA game I ever saw was contested by the Lakers (Minneapolis) and the Pistons (Fort Wayne), and it occurred in Winnipeg.

Being a person from the west, I have to say that I did not, finally, mind relocation, and I have a kind of grudging tolerance for expansion. But I am old enough to recall with fondness the league in which it was honourable to finish in the first division. There is something inescapable tacky about having something called the American League West, in which there are only four teams, and one of them plays in white shoes.

Here is another problem with interleague play. It used to be my bad luck that if I managed to get to a ball game in Seattle or Minnesota the visiting team would be Kansas City. Now I keep seeing them when I get it together to make it to a game in Pittsburgh or San Francisco.

I am getting used to being an old fart, and I no longer get all upset when I mention Eddie Stanky and some young dope with his green Yankees hat on backward says "Who?" But I lie in bed at night imagining that I am the god in charge of baseball. I smile in the dark, observing a world with no interleague play, no wild card, no designated hitter, no sacrifice fly, no Kate Smith, no batting gloves, no scoreboards urging MAKE NOISE, and no high fives for advancing a runner to third by grounding into a double play.

ITALY

One had heard that the finals in the European baseball championship are always between Italy and the Netherlands. Then of course one read Dave Bidini's hilarious book about a season with an Italian second division team, *Baseballissimo*. It mentions, for example, young baseball heroes smoking cigarettes in the dugout while waiting for their mothers to arrive with the tiramisu. That's it, I announced, we have to go to a baseball game in Italy.

So as usual Jean got out the maps, the schedules, the travel brochures and the credit card, and before you could say Giuseppe DiMaggio, we were on our way to the Eternal Stadium. Actually, I thought as we were taking the familiar taxi ride from Leonardo da Vinci airport into Rome, wouldn't it be neat if they could play the Italian all-star game in the Colosseum?

But no, of course not. There is no ball team in Rome, so we had to make do with the Sistine Chapel and such, but then we rented a funny car and headed for Tuscany, where all the other Canadians are. Actually, we went up to the top of a mountain in Tuscany and visited my old friend David Cull and his wife, having dinner outside, of course, next to the pomegranate tree. We were supposed to be at a ball game in Grosseto, but the weekend's play had been suspended while so many young players were at a world university baseball tournament.

I was afraid that our whole trip to Italy had been for naught. We drove into Florence, and though I got to go inside the *Uffizi* and *Il Duomo* for the third or fourth time, I walked past the Botticellis with a heavy heart. But then Jean got out her Blackberry and all that other stuff, and we headed to the train station, across the street from the house in which Shelley wrote *Prometheus Unbound*. I had usually come to Italy in the winter, so I could just walk onto a train. Now the best we could do was reserve two seats in a first class car to Bologna that would get us there after the game has begun. We grabbed them.

According to our city map, the ballpark was as far from the train station as you could get. We got onto a 27A bus, which wended its crooked way through the centre of town, so I pointed out some of the neat stuff Jean could have seen. We got to Gianni Galchi Stadium in the fifth inning, so they charged us five Euros instead of eight. The game, in which Fortitudo dispatched arch enemy Grosseto, was comical. Guys got caught in rundowns because they wanted to be snazzy and swipe bases. Fielders just glanced at grounders because they figured they might be foul. We heard a lot of US rock and roll on the wretched PA, and then at the middle of the seventh inning we heard "Take Me Out to the Ball Game," but no one stood up. What we saw was sort of Class A ball played by individualists.

As soon as the game was over, Jean headed down to the field, and soon I saw her talking to two guys in uniform. Eventually I worked up the nerve to join them. One of them was the manager, who knew only Italian, and the other was the first baseman, who had a Rhode Island accent and, he told us, a wife who spoke only Italian. The manager disappeared for a minute, then came back with the object of Jean's negotiations – the biggest Fortitudo cap he could find. I said thank you in English and Italian, and clapped it onto my head. It was several sizes too small.

But I wear it from time to time.

JACKHAMMERS

I have long been a big fan of minor league baseball and independent league baseball. In fact, as of this writing I have just come back from seeing the inaugural home opener of the Victoria Seals of the Golden Baseball League. They dropped their opener to the Long Beach Armada 6–3.

Yes, among my favourite memories are the details of those hours spent in Christensen Stadium watching the Midland RockHounds, and especially enjoying the two old guys in the stands behind home plate who did the best chicken dance I've ever seen. I think it's now called CitiBank Stadium. That's the way things are going these days. Or watching the Schaumburg Flyers play the Joliet Jackhammers in Schaumburg's Alexian Field, which is next to an airport for small planes that fill the sky above left field, and whose outfield fence is, though constructed from concrete and wood, a replica of nearby Wrigley Field, without the ivy.

Did you know that in St Cloud the relief pitchers are conveyed from the bullpen by Batmobile?

But that brings me to the topic for today. I don't mind the Jackhammers' team name, especially when they have a website punctuated by the appropriate sound. But I am really tired of a certain boring minor league naming trend. The St Cloud team is the River Bats. I am tired of River Bats, River Cats, Bay Cats, River Dogs, Muck Dogs, Sea Dogs, Sand Gnats, Lake Monsters, Iron Pigs, and Fighting Crawdads. The Toledo Mud Hens have been around for over a century, and they have kept their logo longer than anyone in the minors. They are the most famous minor league team in the world. They can stay, but owners in Hoopleville should find a more interesting name. The Lugnuts, for example. The Lookouts.

And don't get me started on teams named after the weather. Forget about the Storm, the Cyclones, the Lightning, the Heat, the Hurricanes. I admire the fantasy team owner who called his team the Humidity.

Here is an unscientific conclusion made about minor league teams. The teams with dumb names (I am not even going to mention the Colorado Springs Sky Sox) such as the Muckdogs usually have bad designs on their caps. You should be able to read a baseball cap from your seat in the grandstand. See the Chicago Cubs. See the New Orleans Zephyrs. But teams like the Muckdogs have to show a snarling dog breaking a baseball bat in its teeth against a background of wigwams and canoes while overhead birds cleave the air. Okay, I exaggerate, but you get my drift. Such messes do not often show up in the major leagues, but a few years back the Toronto cap sported a blue jay, a baseball and a big maple leaf. Now they have replaced that with a big T, though it is the worst T you have ever seen on any athlete.

But just think what some dolt could have done with the Scranton Wilkes Barre Red Barons before they were slurped up by the Yankees.

JACKIE

When I was a kid, say around eleven, the most exciting thing in my life was Jackie Robinson's arrival in the big leagues. It was especially wonderful that he joined my favourite team and got to play with Peewee Reese and Eddie Stanky. Nowadays we say Jack and African American, but in those days we said Jackie and Negro.

In 1945 I was nine, and the newspaper (The Vancouver *Province*) was for watching the Allies march across Europe and hop across the Pacific. I was afraid that when the war ended there would be no more use for a newspaper, but in 1946 I spread it on the floor and read about the Dodgers and the Montreal Royals and Jackie Robinson.

Baseball has never had anything as exciting as Jackie Robinson's arrival in the big leagues. Of course he was the Rookie of the Year in 1947, and the Dodgers won the pennant. In 1949 Jackie led the National League in hitting and was the Most Valuable Player, and the Dodgers won the pennant. Jackie Robinson's Dodgers also won the pennant in 1952, 1953, 1955 and 1956. In 1955 they beat the Yankees at last, and won their first ever World Series. Jackie played third base in that series, and was not the Bums' hitting hero, but he stole home. He stole home in a World Series game! That's what Jackie Robinson used to do.

He was just so damned exciting.

Everyone knows the story about Branch Rickey carefully choosing the fiery Robinson and then urging him to keep cool while he heard the racial catcalls from the stands and the St Louis dugout. Yes, Jackie Robinson was a man of outstanding character and wonderful athletic talent (he had been a college track star and a professional football player), but for me, the important thing was that he was so damned exciting.

Another thing I noticed at the time was that Jackie Robinson was the most handsome man in the National League. I may have just assumed that it was the order of things that he should be, and I may have wondered whether Branch Rickey looked at the Negro Leagues and selected the best-looking man with the most promising statistics. I don't think that I was really an analytical young person. I was more into statistics.

Still, I was uneasy when someone decided to have Jackie Robinson play himself in *The Jackie Robinson Story*. It was made on the cheap and released in 1950, when Jack was thirty-one, and Jack was not a guy who looked younger than his age. They didn't let Rae Robinson play herself, but employed Ruby Dee. And Branch Rickey, a tremendously interesting looking man, was represented by Minor Watson, a guy who usually played the sheriff in Lassie movies.

The movie was okay, I guess, but it wasn't anywhere near as exciting as major league baseball was getting now that Jackie Robinson was here.

JEAN

I don't know how often I have heard a man or a woman tell me "I need a Jean!"

This because he or she has heard me say that Jean plans all the motels, highway routes, ballpark locations and Mexican restaurant availability when we get in the Volvo and head out on a baseball trip. She takes care of tickets and reservations and visas and so on when we go on a cruise or to another continent. I get all embarrassed and confused when I have to talk to publishers and the like, so Jean often gets in between. The income tax guy and the investment guys? Jean.

And I appreciate the hell out of it. Especially when given the added facts that she can cook like a genius, knows how to make a perfect Manhattan, and charmed the acquisitions librarians at the Beinecke and Bancroft libraries, where two of the best collections of my books now rest.

But even more important:

a) she can tell you the infield fly rule, and

b) she knows how to keep score of a baseball game. In fact, I, who was doing that scholarly act when I was eleven, taught her, including the important instruction that you do not enter F7 on a fly ball out unless the left fielder caught it in foul territory. But listen to this: sometimes, in Tucson or Dayton, she will hand me the scorebook while she goes to the Ladies' or to get a couple bratwursts, and I will inevitably screw it up, so that she has to deal with a bunch of crossouts and smudges.

You should hear her insane malicious laughter when Derek Jeter makes a wild throw over the first baseman's head. I would have fallen in love with her for that alone.

Those of you who have been around here for a while will know that Jean is the love interest in my book *Baseball Love*. When I am signing a copy for a baseball nerd who has come out of the woods, I try to get her to sign her name too, but she is too modest. But she was the one who suggested that the publisher (Talonbooks) include my baseball card with each issue. I think she collaborated with them to get the book launch happening in a brewery, where beer and hotdogs were the fare, rather than the usual wine and cheese. Years ago she set things up so that I won an authentic St. Catherines Stompers jersey for winning a baseball trivia contest in southern Ontario.

But mostly I love her for not moving to a seat down the third base line when I get into my admittedly loud antics at the ball park.

JETER

One of the fondest memories we have is the look on Derek Jeter's face right after Luis Gonzales blooped a dinky little pop fly over the drawn-in infield to knock in the winning run and give the Arizona Diamondbacks the 2001 World Series win over the team that thinks it is automatically entitled to the championship. For Jean it was extra sweet because Roger Clemons had been the Yankee starter, and she doesn't care for Roger. She has, furthermore an irrational disregard for Mariano Duncan, often called the premier closer of our time. In this dramatic seventh game of a seesaw World Series Duncan was called on in the eighth, which he got through all right, but in the ninth he committed a throwing error and plunked a batter, which sequence of events was responsible for the drawn-in infield over which Gonzales chipped the final pitch of the series.

But the nicest part of the whole thing, even better than seeing the almost new Arizona franchise win it for the National League, was the look on Jeter's face as he sat in disbelief for a long time before heading for the air conditioning. This just isn't right, that look was saying. I've read the book: it wasn't like this in the book.

Don't get me wrong: I think that Jeter is a good ball player, especially as a hitter and, as they say, a leader. The scuttlebutt is that as a fielder he ranks low in the scale of MLB shortstops, but the moment I will in all fairness recall also occurred in the 2001 postseason. On October 13, in the third game of the American League Divisional Series against Oakland (don't we just *hate* these things?) the shortstop retrieved a live ball somewhere on the first base line and while his body hurtled toward the Yankee dugout, flipped the ball to catcher Jorge Posada, who tagged out Jeremy Giambi and saved the Yanks from elimination. It was such an electrifying play that you can't just dial it up, because it's been copyrighted by some scrounge outfit.

But let's go back to Derek Jeter's face. It is a very nice colour because his father's roots go back to Africa and his mother's to northern Europe. But he always seems to be sneering. As in I am so fuckin' good. He is the Kobe Bryant of baseball, without the behaviour that gets you into the courts and the tabloids. The infielder who plays to his right has that beautiful colour in his face, but he's a regular in the tabloids at least. We like it when he screws up on the field, but it's Jeter we like to see throw the ball two meters above the first baseman's glove.

It's partly because he is the captain of the Yankees. But we never had anything against Willie Randolph. As of 2008 Jeter was driving a Ford Escape, which is what they call an SUV crossover, but the guy who plays to his right was driving a Hummer. That's a *real* jerk car. Well, he is what the entertainment people call a "notorious bachelor." But Jesus was a bachelor. Uh oh.

I think it's mainly the sneer. But Elvis Presley wore a sneer, and people just loved him even before he was dead. Well, *I* didn't like him. And I wonder: if Derek Jeter were playing shortstop for the Cincinnati Reds would I turn my animus toward, say, Johnnie Damon, that traitor?

86

JOKERS

In national and international politics I lean well to the left. That is, I oppose just about all of the governments that the US has installed around the world. In baseball I am what is called a conservative, or better a traditionalist. That is, I don't like the Designated Hitter, as I may have mentioned, don't like the sacrifice fly, don't much care for names on the backs of shirts, don't like the five-man rotation and the pitch count, can do without that pitcher stat called a "hold."

But here is one way in which I differ from the unsmiling coots who like haircuts and neckties: I like ballplayers with a sense of humour. I like flakes and jokers and oddballs. Don't get me wrong – most ballplayers are pretty dumb and have pretty dumb ideas about what is funny. Shaving cream pies in the face are what I am talking about here. The hotfoot. The typical rookie-hazing clichés. Compare the silent treatment when a puny infielder returns to the dugout after hitting a three-run homer – now *that's* funny.

After Casey Stengel was traded from the Dodgers to the Pirates he would catch it from the Ebbets Field fans, so once he came to the plate in Brooklyn, doffed his cap to the crowd, and released a sparrow that had been under it. The fans stopped booing and started cheering, even though they had been given the bird. The glum-faced Pittsburgh owners traded him to Philadelphia for a guy named Possum Whitted.

Baseball owners and general managers and most managers do not like a ballplayer with wit. They want Derek Jeter or Cal Ripkin. The only reason that Bill Lee didn't get traded twice a year is that he was a left-handed pitcher with control. He hated AstroTurf and polyester, and claimed to carry a Yankee catcher's baseball card in his back pocket so that said Yankee would have his face up against the Spaceman's ass at all times. He was in favour of health food and health smoke, and was just plain ten times more interesting than a rotation full of Don Suttons. He was the most interesting Red Sox player after Jim Piersall.

When I was a teenager I was crazy, as they say, about Jim Piersall. I wish there had been television so that I could have seen the outfield I loved. I could have watched Piersall walking behind Dom DiMaggio and imitating the Little Professor's peculiar gait. Who could not love a singles hitter who ran the bases facing backward after hitting his hundredth home run as an antiquated member of the New York Mets? He was dealt to the Angels a few weeks later, and was soon to enter my nonconformist's hall of fame. On road trips I room him with Jim Bouton.

K

When I was in the Kosmik League in my thirties, and later in the Twilight League until I retired after breaking my hip in 2003, I was known as a guy who could get the bat on the ball. I was not known as a home run threat, and in fact in my sixties I had to leg it to first to avoid getting thrown out by an outfielder who had picked up my sure single. But I could get through a season on a ration of about five or six strikeouts.

I had a good eye. I knew how to foul off questionable pitches. I was an expert on the rules and the details. So if I did strike out I felt terrible. *Give me one more chance!* The worst feeling of all is to be called for a third strike on a pitch that you know absolutely was low, or high, or way outside. You are standing there with a dangerous stick in your hands, but you are totally emptied of possibility. I think that being called out on a third strike that was not a strike is worse than hitting into a double play. It is worse than being thrown out of church when it was someone else that blew the loud fart.

I think that it must feel pretty good to be Randy Johnson and to know that the batter is thinking that he could be a strikeout victim in a minute or so. But on the occasions when I was a relief pitcher I felt just as good in inducing a ground ball as I did in whiffing the guy, though I have to admit that the latter was not a frequent occurrence.

As in infielder, which I normally was (and how sad this is to be writing in the past tense), I was not a big fan of the strikeout, though I would shout encouragement to Gordon (Excruciating) Payne or whoever our chucker was, and I would exhibit pep in the resultant around the horn. As an infielder one likes to see a ground ball, to set one's body into the rhythm of that nicely-timed erasure. It must have been an honour of sorts for Mickey Morandini, playing second base for the Cubs against Houston at Wrigley Field on May 6, 1998, as Kerry Wood pitched one of the greatest games in National League history. The Astros got one hit, and one batsman reached after being plunked by Wood, but the Cubs' young pitcher struck out twenty batters, only the second pitcher to do such a thing. Roger Clemens struck out twenty Mariners one day in 1986, but gave up a run on three hits, and struck out twenty Tigers one day in 1996, but gave up five hits. Mickey Morandini got to stand near second base all through the greatest strikeout game ever pitched.

All right, that was probably pretty exciting, in a boring kind of way. But fifteen years earlier, in a game against St. Louis, the previous Cubs second baseman had a pretty exciting game at Wrigley himself. On June 12, 1983, Ryne Sandberg had twelve assists against the Cardinals to tie the major league record for second basemen. As a spectator I would have preferred to see Wood's game; as a second baseman I would have preferred to be in the earlier one.

But not if the home plate umpire struck me out on a pitch off the plate.

KINER

It will be a little hard to explain how I felt about the phenomenon of Ralph Kiner in 1949, when I was thirteen years old. If you knew that I preferred Gene Autry to Roy Rogers, Ty Cobb to Babe Ruth, the National League to the American League, you would know that I preferred players with good batting averages to home run kings. I was a fan of Richie Ashburn, who used to get about two homers a year, hitting leadoff for the Phils. He always got more putouts than Willy Mays did, but his highest homer season was his last one with the Mets, when he got seven. The second highest was four, so you see what I mean.

Ralph Kiner was quoted as saying that home run hitters drive Cadillacs. This was back when you did not get a ten million dollar salary for batting .260. Kiner led the National League in homers seven years in a row, I think. The sportswriters went gaga. Here was a guy who hit over fifty twice, back when you had to do that without chemistry. Despite Johnny Mize and Hank Greenberg, I associated home runs with the American League. In the National league we knew how to bunt. We had Richie Ashburn and Eddie Stanky, who were pictured bunting on their baseball cards. We stole home in a cloud of dirt. We had right-handed hitters who went the other way to hit behind the runner. Where did this Ralph Kiner come from? Why wasn't he playing for the Tigers or the Athletics?

But in later years I felt better toward Kiner than I did in 1950, when Richie Ashburn led the Whiz Kids to the first Phillies pennant since 1915, while Kiner's Pirates, despite his 47 home runs, finished eighth and last. But you know, the Pirates finished third in attendance that year, just barely behind the Phils.

Here is why I feel better toward Kiner now. The tradeoff is supposed to be home run hitting against high average. But look: Babe Ruth had a .342 lifetime batting average, and Ted Williams hit .344. Ralph Kiner's all-around hitting doesn't look all that bad when you compare him to later home run kings. Much was made at the time of the fact that Kiner averaged 80 strikeouts a season, and the idea of giving up whiffs for bombs became part of the game.

But if you compare Kiner's totals with later swingers, you might be tempted to think of him as a Richie Ashburn with power. In 2008 Jack Cust struck out 197 times! He walked 111 times. In over half his plate appearances he did not hit the ball fair. Cust is a record-holder (he was on my fantasy team for a few months), but he is the poster boy for a trend.

He hit .231 and got 33 homers in 2008, and is still employed. That is the way baseball has changed since 1949, and that is why I feel better toward Ralph Kiner than I once did. My fantasy team would not have put him on waivers, that's for sure.

KING

Okay, here is the reason for my liking Stephen King, the bestselling horror author. I believe that he has a season ticket at Fenway Park, and that he is so rich that it's okay if he just uses it once in a while. The reason I like him is that he brings a book to the games, and reads a few pages while the teams are moving from field to dugout or *vice versa* between innings. If I attend a game alone I do that as well. It's an extension of what I do at home, reading in front of the ballgame on TV. And if the game is between the Angels and Rangers I just might continue reading *during* the innings as well.

I have never read a novel by Stephen King. Nor by Dean Koontz, Sidney Sheldon, Nora Roberts, John Grisham, Richard Ludlum or Anne Rice. I'm the outsider in the airport departure lounge, me and my Joseph Conrad.

But I have seen some of the frothy movies made from Stephen King books, and I have read half a book by Stephen King. It is called *Faithful: Two Diehard Boston Red Sox Fans Chronicle the Historic 2004 Season*. The other diehard fan was Stewart O'Nan, an author, I would more recently find, of several novels about unhappiness and murder. The two writers follow the Bosox from spring training to the sensational playoffs and the World Series sweep of the Cardinals.

O'Nan is the better of the two chroniclers. I was surprised by the low quality of Stephen King's writing. I knew that he was immensely popular, that his novels are guaranteed best sellers, but I had thought that he might almost be as good, say, as Elmore Leonard. But no, he just comes across as an ordinary ball fan, the kind of guy you might see watching a game on his back deck television set. His writing is not clever, not funny, tending toward low-energy clichés of a person who doesn't read much.

Yet, he does read a lot, and I once heard that he reviewed poetry under another name, and he does take a book to the ballpark. It may be just a James Patterson book, but there he sits in his round glasses, reading a book outdoors in the evening, and that's good enough for me.

I mean there he is setting a good example. There are enough bad examples around, among pop culture role models. A hip-hop star named Kanye West recently explained why there is no room for books in his life. He said that he learns all he has to know from talking with people he meets on the street and elsewhere. Apparently both his parents are or were professors. So much for the old idea that raising your kid with books around the house will ensure intellectual curiosity.

But maybe, just maybe, if the other 39,927 spectators at Fenway would read books between innings, some of the ballplayers would take the wires out of their ears and read books, if just, say, *The Shining*.

KIYOOKA

The marvelous artist Roy Kiyooka was born on the prairies, and when he was a little Japanese-sized kid he was the water boy for a champion women's softball team.

The great writer Robert Kroetsch was born on the prairies, and when the grown men were overseas fighting the Krauts he got to be a teenage first baseman on the local baseball team.

The terrific poet Lionel Kearns was born in Nelson, BC, but his family moved to the prairies so his father could train pilots to fight the Krauts, and Lionel became a good hockey player and a pretty darn good third baseman.

The sensational novelist Jack Kerouac was not born on the prairies, but when I was living on the prairies I read many of his books, and when I read about his childhood made-up baseball game, I recalled that when I was a kid I had a made-up baseball game too.

The splendid painter Dorothy Knowles was born on the prairies, and has provided many beautiful big pictures of the prairies in all weathers and seasons and colours. She doesn't put people in her landscapes, so never portrays baseball players.

The popular novelist Joy Kogawa was a youngster in one of the many Japanese-Canadian families that were robbed of their west coast property and moved to concentration camps in eastern BC and the prairies. The young men in these camps played excellent baseball, often against teams of European-Canadian lads.

The amusing poet Kenneth Koch is known as a member of the New York School of poets. Most of the younger poets of the New York school were from the prairies, but Koch was born in Cincinnati. His breakthrough book, *Ko, or a Season on Earth*, (1959) is about a Japanese baseball star and takes place partly in Kalamazoo.

Roy Kiyooka played rover on a hockey team when he was a kid on the frozen prairie where you could not expect to see kyogen in the theatre.

Robert Kroetsch had trouble hitting the knuckleball. Never mind the ump, he thought, kill the pitcher.

Lionel Kearns went to school in the West Kootenay, learning the saxophone and bagpipes and fishing for kokonee.

Jack Kerouac used to be called King of the Beats when really what he wanted was to understand the law of Karma.

Dorothy Knowles went to Emma Lake, where Clement Greenberg kissed her and encouraged her to make landscapes.

Joy Kogawa's family moved to the prairies after the war, and she went to school there, east of Kicking Horse.

Kenneth Koch went on to engage in a second career, teaching kids how to write poems.

KOSMIK

In the early seventies Vancouver and environs were filled with artists, especially young artists, and lots of people who did something pretty close to what the artists were doing. It was also a time when Pierre Trudeau's government was looking for ways to promote a kind of thoughtful patriotism, which was kind of interesting, given that places like Vancouver were loaded with US Americans coming up to live where the government wasn't interested in bombing Asians. Trudeau's government set up two nifty programs involving grants: Local Initiative Programs (LIP) and Opportunities for Youth (OFY). I can't really remember which one the Kosmik League fell under, but wasn't that a neat thing? The federal government gave young Vancouverites money to buy softball equipment and pay for playing space.

And from the get-go the KL acted as a kind of parody of organized baseball. The names of the teams ran from highly comic to abysmally low comic. My team of painters and poets was called the Granville Grange Zephyrs, in honour of the building under the Granville Street Bridge wherein our first baseman and ace pitcher had their studios. But there were teams called The Flying Dildos (they couldn't have had any poets), the Afghani Oil Kings, the East End Punks, and my favourite – a women's team called Nine Easy Pieces. We all, though lots of us had sheer athletic talent, treated softball as theatre.

Some of it was minimalist, or you could call it stupid. If the Zeds were twenty runs ahead of a team such as the Mental Patients Society's Napoleons (whose team shirts showed a hand tucked inside) we would call for the double steal – in which the guy on first stole second while the guy on second stole first. Or if the bases were loaded, the triple steal, at the end of which all three base runners would slide into the pitcher's rubber. Any teenage lad who dared to get on base against Nine Easy Pieces was on his own – his teammates might have a sip or a toke while he was ganged by the whole infield. There was one team whose catcher always played totally wrapped in white bandage, like the guy in the movie of *The Invisible Man*.

I have told the story of the Kosmik League elsewhere, so I will not review its history here. I just want to mention how much I miss it, how happy I was in the early seventies (which were, as you know, still the sixties) to play at Daisy Beanblossom Stadium in a game that let a person handle a ground ball perfectly but also to do something utterly silly in the next inning, to be as good a player as he or she can be, but to make much-needed ridicule of both Little League and career-planning.

There was the odd career-planner in the league. Sometimes one of these gents would dispute an out call because he was tagged five seconds after he had reached the bag at third – and furthermore that he had been tagged not with the game ball but with a beachball that had been tossed to the third baseman by his girlfriend on the sidelines. Out for not being Kosmik enough. Out for wearing a shirt with a little alligator on it. Safe for handing the umpire a chocolate-chip oatmeal cookie.

LITERATURE

Charyn, Jerome. *The Seventh Babe*, New York, Arbor House, 1979, 352pp. This is my favourite baseball novel of all time, and the first Charyn book I ever read. If I had to be a US novelist, I'd like to be Charyn.

Clark, Tom. *One Last Round for the Shuffler*, New York, Truck Books, 1979, 157pp. What happens when a spitballer's money pitch is made illegal.

Dawson, Fielding. *A Great Day for a Ballgame*, Indianapolis, Bobbs-Merrill, 1973, 151pp. Fee Dawson, in more than one book, beautifully caught the connection between baseball and sexual love.

DeLillo, Don. *Pafko at the Wall*, New York, Scribner, 2001, 96pp. Included in *Underworld*. A fine novella published on the fiftieth anniversary of that infamous game in which Bobby Thomson killed the Dodgers' pennant dream.

Hall, Donald. *Fathers Playing Catch with Sons*, Farrar, Straus and Giroux, 1984, 208pp. Here's a poet I used to imagine as my enemy, with whom I sat by the river in Cleveland and talked baseball all afternoon.

Kinsella, W.P. *The Thrill of the Grass*, Toronto, Penguin, 1984, 208pp. This guy could not throw or hit, but he knew that baseball helps people get over the sheer awfulness of life.

Lardner, Ring. *You Know Me Al*. New York, Doran, 1916, 224pp. This is the writer who showed me when I was a teenager that you could be a writer and still dig baseball.

Oppenheimer, Joel. *The Wrong Season*, Indianapolis, Bobbs-Merrill, 1973, 165pp. The great New York poet and columnist endures a year at Shea Stadium.

Richler, Mordecai. *St. Urbain's Horseman*, Toronto, McClelland & Stewart, 1971, 467pp. Contains the much-anthologized "Playing Ball on Hampstead Heath."

Roth, Philip. *The Great American Novel*, New York, Holt, Rinehart and Winston, 1973, 382pp. In which baseball is seen to be every bit as comical as the country in which it is most often played.

Sorrentino, Gilbert. *The Imaginative Qualities of Actual Things*, New York, Pantheon, 1971, 243pp. New York poet and novelist deconstructs the place of baseball in people's lives and makes it plainer than ever before.

Thurber, James. *My World – And Welcome to It*, New York, Harcourt, Brace, 1942, 234pp. Contains the Lardneresque "You Could Look it Up."

Tolnay, Tom (ed.). *Baseball and the Lyrical Life*, Delhi, NY, Birch Book Press, 1999, 88pp. One of the best collections of baseball poems.

Williams, William Carlos. *White Mule*. Norfolk, New Directions, 1937, 293pp. The legendary US poet provides a memorable and accurate account of an afternoon at the Polo Grounds.

LITTLE

I have mixed feelings about Little League, that's for sure. I'm glad that the kids are on that greenery learning the great game, even though some of their coaches are dads filled with misconceptions. But when I see these kids with their batting gloves and expensive shoes and after-game pizzas, I am nostalgic for the days of sandlot/pickup baseball.

Carl Stotz started Little League in Williamsport, Pennsylvania in

1939, but it had not reached Oliver by the time that I was of appropriate age (5 to 18), and the closest we came was something called Junior Baseball. The first Little League outside the USA was formed in British Columbia in 1951, but that, like so many other things, happened down at the Coast. When I left Oliver in 1953, there were rumours that Little League was coming to town.

Now Little League is all over the world, and teams from Asia and Latin America compete in the Little League World Series, which is a tournament held in South Williamsport and shown on television every year. The organizers arrange the playoffs so that the final game has to have a US team in it.

Such organization reached Oliver in time for my kid brother Jim to become a star pitcher and hitter. I came home to watch him play in the summer of 1962, just after he had turned thirteen. I was not to play any ball at all between the ages of sixteen and nineteen, when I toiled at second base for the RCAF Macdonald Rocketeers. I kept a toothpick in my mouth, just in case there were some curious photographers and reporters among the 14 people who watched our games.

So I never did get all the organized youth baseball clear in my mind. What were the ages, etcetera, for Babe Ruth ball, Connie Mack ball, American Legion ball, and so on? Looking back, I sort of wish that I had had the Little League experience, though I find it hard to picture my having a proper glove and proper spikes and all. On the other hand, I know that being quirky and unconventionally intelligent would have been discouraged, and I might have been kept on the bench by some dad who did not know who Al Zarilla was. Still, unorganized ball had its shortcomings. At least in Little League they probably didn't have the inevitable little genius who declared "five foul balls and you're out," or "a tie goes to the runner."

But I will never shake the feeling that organized kids' baseball is a little like a girls' camp I recently heard about. Apparently at this camp they teach ten-year-old girls how to be executives' wives, how to chat with their husband's boss, how to provide a career-enhancing dinner for six, and so on. In the US all the Little League games are played against a backdrop of US flags, and you see a lot of little outfielders with ads for local plumbers and hardware stores on their backs.

LOGAN

Every second week, Jean and I drive out to Surrey to have lunch with my childhood pal Willy, who is now blind, and who never knew a thing about baseball anyway. We have this lunch, which we call GBAD, which is short for Great Breakfast All Day, for reasons that would take too long to tell you, in a pub called the Newton Arms. It's one of those places that fancies itself a sports bar, with lots of television sets tuned to poker games and ultimate fighting, hockey jerseys and goalie sticks on the walls, and so on. On the wall just outside the men's john there are some framed sports photos, mainly the usual. The one I look at every time I head for a pee is a picture of Johnny Logan.

If you have been reading since the chapters that start with A, you'll know that I pride myself on knowing that it's Johnny Logan, and assuming that no one else in the joint would know. I went and checked the picture today. Johnny Logan is between Hank Aaron and Eddie Mathews. They are wearing that nice rich Milwaukee Braves uniform from the fifties, probably 1957, the championship year.

What I mean is, I wonder whether if I were twenty years old now, would I recognize a picture of Casey Blake a half century from now? Or let's put it another way: would Johnny Logan's picture be there if he were not smiling between two hall of famers? Okay – I figure that some of the men heading for a leak will recognize hank Aaron, and maybe once in a while some old gent might think: is that Eddie Mathews? But I'll bet that Johnny Logan's name, even if he did have those big expressive eyes and even if he did play short for a pennant-winning team in Wisconsin, just doesn't register.

But partly that's me. I would have recognized Allie Reynolds,

Bobby Schantz, Andy Pafko or Sandy Amoros. And being an old fart, I probably remember their names better than I do the lineup of the Kansas City Royals today. Maybe this is because when I was twenty you kept track of the ballplayers in newspapers and magazines, whereas today they are just bits of light on a television screen.

The name was something. Johnny Logan. It's the kind of name you might make up for a boy's novel about baseball, or for a drive-in movie star, like Tab Hunter. It could have been "Johnny Logan, Private Eye," or "Johnny Logan, Young Middleweight." Even when I was twenty I was a little suspicious. Johnny Logan even had those big eyes, curly shiny black hair and general almost moist gleam that male starlets had in the Eisenhower years.

LOGOS

When I am in my poetry mode I consider the Logos, and place my poor talent in the hands of a divine order, whatever reckoning, the word of God, for example, or the gods. It's only logical, this faith.

But when I am in my baseball mode, "logos" becomes plural, and we are not dealing with the rule of the universe at all. If there is any spirit involved, he is likely to be what Jack Spicer the baseball fan poet called a "low ghost." A logo is properly not a combination of river cats, chewed baseball bats and flags; it is a letter or a few letters designating what is essentially a company of sportsmen. It is to my sorrow that the best one in the business belongs to that outfit that has stolen so much else in my world, the New York Yankees.

But before we depart from the subject of philosophy and ball caps, I would like to mention my favourite ball cap logo if we are talking about irony and other humour. An old friend of mine from the Calgary days is Ed Hunnert, a philosophy professor who wound up at University Of British Columbia, where he was a thoughtful star on the Philosophy Department ball team. Their cap, he told me, was grey, and affixed to the front was a grey on grey letter O with wings.

It signified the Owls, avian symbols of wisdom, of course, mysterious messengers of the Logos, if you are an ancient Athenian, where Plato and that crowd started the stuff.

Everyone has a logo now. Beer labels look something like ball caps. Any time an athlete or coach or owner is interviewed on television, someone has hung a curtain of logos behind this person. In the strange game called soccer the players just say the hell with it and wear a company logo on their shirts instead of a team name. I used to root for Commodore and Opel, but now my money and sympathies are with Novotel. I keep track of AIG's scores too.

It's a little harder to be a fan in Swedish hockey. The players wear about eight company names on their outfits, the ice and boards are a riot of commercial messages, and even the goalposts have advertisements on them. And don't even mention those car races that yokels in the South love so much – the cars and the drivers of the cars look like downtown Tokyo. I think they have logos on their logos.

So far baseball has had the decency not to have a bank's name on the players' chests. It's bad enough that stadiums are now named after loan companies and pet food dispensers, and I have to say that I was blessed to become a baseball fan during that lovely time when the fences back of major league outfields did not have pecuniary words all over them. In fact I used to think that it was kind of nifty to see that ad for a gasoline company outside Fenway Park.

I am also happy that baseball doesn't show you a lot of bare skin, so that we don't get those moronic tattoos that characterize professional basketball along with the gangster music. I have always liked the tangle of letters on the Cardinals' cap, but I don't want to see it on skin.

LOWELL

I went with Ed Pechter our center fielder to Lowell in 1970, looking for Jack Kerouac's newish grave, but though I asked for and got directions to the Canuck graveyard, and though we saw all the Quebec names we were used to, we didn't find Jack because he didn't have a stone yet. But we did get to Fenway and we did see the Sox beat Ed's Yankees 8–4, I think it was.

In 2005 my baseball love and I were on a tour in a rented car that took us from Toronto to Montreal by way of Bras d'Or, Nova Scotia. Our plan included seeing as many games as possible in the parks of the Red Sox system. It went well at first, as we saw Pawtucket host the Buffalo Bisons on August 9th. But then things went awry. Bad news, said Jean – we can't make the game in Brockton. Aw shucks, I replied. Because we have tickets for the sold-out game at Fenway, she finished. If you have read my book about Jean and baseball, you will not be surprised that she managed this, nor even that my name was printed on the tickets.

Okay, excellent. The Red Sox hit as many home runs as the White Sox did, and won the game 9–8, a typical Fenway score and yet another reason I keep falling in love with this babe. But I want you to know that she isn't perfect. We arrived at the stadium in Lynn, only to find out that the North Shore Spirit had played one of their season's two day games in the steam heat that afternoon. I should remind you that the same thing happened in Missoula a couple years earlier, but at least that time we got to go to a game there the following night. And the Lynn debacle was ameliorated by the fact that the Spirit were not a Red Sox farm team but a member of the independent Can Am League.

But next day we did get to sit inside LeLacheur Stadium in Lowell, where the temperature was 95 degrees F. and the humidity was about the same as that on Venus. We had bought tickets for some blazing sun field, but a complete stranger gave us her tickets in the shade back of third, and we were there in time to get two free Paul Revere bobble head dolls. Unfortunately, the Oneonta Tigers clobbered the Spinners.

The city of Lowell had been transformed since my last visit. The old black mills with broken windowpanes had been cleaned and sandblasted in some federal reclamation project, and best of all, the Kerouac monument at Bridge and French was unvisited save by us, and I got to read his marvelous words carved in marble stones and reimagine the Lowell celebrated in his novels. We also went to the Stations of the Cross celebrated in his books, and I brought home an abandoned bird's nest with a feather in it. It is in front of my face right now, alongside the trophy I won for having the best team in my fantasy league in 1996.

The next day we were supposed to catch a Class Double-A game in Portland, but the night before it looked as if there was not a room available in the whole state of Maine. Luckily again, at 1:30 AM a guy running a motel in South Portland phoned a motel in Waterville, eighty miles north, and we abandoned all hope of seeing the Sea Dogs play, choosing a bed instead.

So New England was not perfect. But it was wonderful, which is better.

MAYS

When I was just out of high school there was no baseball on television, not where I was living, anyway. And I didn't live anywhere near a major league baseball park, so I did not see a MLB game till I was 31, a year after my first trip to Europe. So if I wanted to know what was going on in the majors, I had to depend on sports pages and sports magazines. I was hoping to write for them one day, so I paid attention to how the "scribes" wrote – Shirley Povich, Bob Broeg, Grantland Rice.

In the early fifties the baseball writers, whether they worked in New York or not, were agreed that three of the all-time great center fielders were playing their home games in that city, one in Brooklyn, one in Harlem, and one in the Bronx. By 1980 all three were in the Hall of Fame, but three decades later pretty well anyone agrees that Willie Mays was the best, Mickey Mantle was second best, and Duke Snider was pretty damned good. Larry Doby and Richie Ashburn made it to Cooperstown too.

In fact a lot of people say that Willie Mays was the best player ever. Here was a guy who hit 660 home runs, but the most famous photograph of him shows him halfway through the most renowned fielding play in World Series history. Think about how impressive this is: it is usually referred to as "the catch." Do we have anything referred to as "the hit" or "the throw" or "the slide"? Willie was the epitome of the five-skill ballplayer. He was born the same year as Mantle was, 1931. They both reached the majors in 1951. They were both five feet eleven inches tall.

But Willie got 868 more hits than Mantle did, 124 more homers, 185 more stolen bases. He outhit him by four percentage points. He got twenty-two home runs in extra innings, making him dramatic as well as efficient. He missed all of the 1953 season and almost all of the season before that, to military service. In the two seasons after he was mustered out he got 92 homers! I am among those who believe that if he had played for the Giants in 1952–3, he would have hit at least 80 home runs, passing Babe Ruth and then some.

As I recall, Mickey Mantle got more ink before he made it to New York and for a while afterward. But we know that that's because he was a Yankee. In 1951 Willy Mays won the National League rookie award, but Gil McDougald the Yankee won the American League one, despite the fact that the Chicago White Sox had Minnie Miñoso, a black Cuban who beat McDougald at nearly everything, including batting (.324 to .306) and OPS (.917 to .884).

Was Major League baseball going to give both its rookie awards to Black players in 1951? Not likely. Miñoso's stats had Mays's stats beaten all to hell, but Orestes was a foreigner and Willie was the "Say Hey Kid." He was always smiling. He was great in the clubhouse, said Mr. Durocher. If the USA was going to let Negroes onto the set, they'd better have a personality that didn't seem too serious. They'd better not be Curt Flood.

But Willie? Oh, I wish he had smiled that bright smile while showing the photographers a baseball with the number 715 on it.

MILWAUKEE

I have thrown the first pitch before games in Grand Forks, Welland and Vancouver, but my favourite was at Miller Park in Milwaukee. I love those Millers. My grandmother's maiden name was Miller. My brother's wife's name was Miller. In Milwaukee, my catcher was Damian Miller. There's an M for you.

It started when the University of Wisconsin at Milwaukee, and then the best poetry store in the USA, Woodland Pattern, invited me to town for a couple of readings. I said sure, okay, because I had never been to Milwaukee and I like seeing new cities. But I bargained: I'll come if it happens during baseball season, I said, and the Brewers are at home. We'll get right on it, they said, especially Susan Firer, the Milwaukee poet.

And so they did. What I didn't know was that they were going to talk to the Brewers and see what they could do to bring poetry and baseball together where they are supposed to be. So they set up my first National League appearance, and they set up a party in my honour at the big Miller brewery. Phew, I said, how about a visit to the riverside home of the great Wisconsin poet Lorine Niedecker? Can do, they said.

But that did it. Riding in the back seat out to Fort Atkinson and Black Hawk Island, I got sick as I sometimes did before seeing Chris, my physical therapy guy, so I threw up in the Fort Atkinson library, threw up again in the Fort Atkinson museum, peering at Niedecker relics through my dizziness and headache. The island was neat, but I threw up on the wet ground.

When we got back to Milwaukee I went straight to my bed in the Irish pub, and begged off the party at the brewery, but made them promise to pick me up for the ball game against the Reds. Thank goodness I had been all right for the readings the day before, especially because I shared the bookstore reading with Ammiel Alcalay, whom I had been reading of late.

At the ballpark I sat as still as I could, waiting for my moment, sick as a dog, sick as a Lake Michigan sea dog. A couple minutes before game time my posse got me to the right gate, and out on the magnificent field I went, suddenly clear of mind, ready to go. I was like one of those wonderful old jazz musicians that wake up from the dead off stage to wail for two hours. My name was up on the JumboTron. I threw a strike low on the outside corner and got the ball signed by Mr. Miller. Then I headed back to my seat along the third base line. On the way I stopped for one of the reasons a person has always wanted to go to a game in Milwaukee, a signature bratwurst, yes, with sauerkraut.

It was yummy. I had missed the party, after all. I threw it up in a waste bin before taking my seat to endure the game.

MONTREAL

Here is my stupid fate: I have been an intense baseball aficionado for my whole life, but I have lived 96% of that time in places that do not boast a major league baseball team. When I moved back to Vancouver in 1971, I was glad that there was a Triple-A team here, and thought that maybe we would get a MLB team someday soon. Unfortunately we fell to Single-A, and though I follow the Canadians faithfully, and intertwine my life with theirs in several ways, I rue my stupid fate as defined above.

As you who know arithmetic will understand, I spent 4% of my life in a big league town. Sort of. I was living in Montreal when the Expos came to town. "Expos" was a nice word to say, but it was the stupidest name ever for a major league ball team, one of the reasons for my "sort of" above. Another was Parc Jarry, where the Expos played. It was a small all-aluminum stadium with no grandstand roof. It just did not, though the Saint Louis Cardinals and Bob Gibson were out there on the grass and dirt, look or feel like a big league building. And on the days when the Expos handed out miniature baseball bats to all the kids, it did not *sound* like a major league building, what with all those bats whanging the aluminum seats.

That was an example of Montreal verve, of *éclat*. French-speaking Montrealers with their Gallic emotionality sometimes do things that make the rest of us cringe, we Anglos with our quiet good taste. But at other times, especially when in the presence of visiting us Americans, we are proud or at least fond of the Quebecois *daringness*. At Parc Jarry, which was a subway ride plus a bus ride into the east end, there was a guy who often bought a seat for his pet duck. There was another guy who used to take his violin to the park, so that at least once during the game he could stand on the Expos' dugout roof and fiddle.

Sometimes, not often enough now that I think back, I went to the game with novelist Hugh Hood or short story writer Clark Blaise. In the spirit of the place I would cheer loudly and bilingually, "Frappez one, le Grande Orange!" That last was the nickname for outfielder Rusty Staub, the first Little Leaguer to become a major league star.

Once my parents came from the Okanagan Valley in British Columbia, and I took my father to the only major league ball game he would ever see, this a guy who was a Cardinals fan when Rogers Hornsby was their first baseman. At 5'11" Hornsby and my dad were pretty tall for their time. I can't remember what visiting team we saw, or who won, but I do remember feeling that it was not right that this great fan and ball player should have had to wait till he was in his sixties to see a MLB game, and then had to see it in such a hick stadium.

By 1980, playing their home games in ill-fated Olympic Stadium, the Montreal Expos were the best team in baseball. Next year they made it to post-season play due to the strike, and then they began to fall back, becoming a so-so team in a dank edifice with a retractable roof that would not open. Concrete fell from time to time, but there were so few fans that no one was hit. Jean and I went to a game there during the last season, and saw that although the crowd was sparse, it was knowledgeable and loud. But Montreal is a notoriously front-running town, and unless your team is a winner you might have to disband (football) or move to Washington (baseball).

Still, I wish they were here in Vancouver.

MOVIES

Sometimes you feel ironically nostalgic about the baseball movies of your childhood and youth, but baseball movies are a lot better than they used to be. There are still some pretty bad movies about baseball (see "Angels in the Outfield" or "Mr. 3000") but I think that we can agree that the imaginations in Hollywood are a lot better than they used to be.

When we were kids we had to see the baseball movies, no matter how bad we thought the last one was. Maybe I should use the first person singular here. I had to see Ronald Reagan as Grover Cleveland Alexander, even though I had just seen Dan Dailey as Dizzy Dean. Was the dancer chosen to play the pitcher because of the alliterative D?

In those days, say 1952, the main idea the screen people had was to make a film out of some (usually retired) major leaguer's career. I figure the thought was that movies were about American heroes, and so was baseball, so naturally anyone with a natural American appetite would go to a flick about Lou Gehrig or Monty Stratton, especially if there was a fatal disease or an amputation to deal with. If you weren't going to make this kind of inspirational story, as when Grover Cleveland Alexander overcomes alcoholism, you would go for the other option – comedy. So there was an Abbot and Costello film, and "who's on first?" became as famous a saying as "don't shoot until you see the whites of their eyes." But generally speaking the comedies were more imaginative and otherwise better than the biographies. One of the best ideas was "It Happens Every Spring," (1949) in which a fuddy-duddy inventor creates a substance that repels wood, and the St. Louis ball team succeeds wildly.

But as in most of the baseball movies of mid-century, the actors did not know how to throw a ball and the director seemed to be an American who had never seen a game. In this film the director was not allowed to use any real team nicknames on the uniforms, because Commissioner of Baseball Happy Chandler didn't want to be seen as encouraging "cheating," so you see that the baseball people were as dopy as the movie people. I guess the two worlds *were* meant for each other in the Eisenhower years.

But even though I loved baseball and Randolph Scott, I had become a cynic the year before, when "The Babe Ruth Story" came out, with William Bendix as the Babe. Oh boy. Well, the film looked as if it had been made in one week at a cost of a few thousand clams, so who could expect much? I mean, I had seen a Johnny Mack Brown western or two. But these dunces had now cast William Bendix as Babe Ruth. No twelve-year old could look at that and not begin to suspect that phoniness penetrated right down to the bottom of everything they offered you for money. The awkwardly moving fake dinosaurs of the sci-fi black-and-whites might as well have been playing the outfield in this travesty.

I think I might have known a couple years later how Jimmy Piersall felt when the man that Ted Williams called the best-fielding outfielder he had ever seen was portrayed on television by Tab Hunter and then on the big screen by Tony Perkins.

MUSIC

I will be going out on a limb here, and maybe not for the first time. And I will not be discussing the bozo outfielder who takes his boom box into the clubhouse and imposes his loud taste on his teammates, thus garnering the reputation of a morale-booster. I mean to talk about the music favoured by fans. And here I am not referring, either, to the strains of the "Chicken Dance" that get me and George Stanley up on our feet and pinching the air.

Professional basketball has marketted itself as part of the world of Black USAmerican gangster clothing, tattoos and hip-hop music. A lot of rap videos feature basketball action along with the big female bums and guys with hats crooked on their heads. Steve Nash stands out in this milieu because he has no tats and no diamond in his ear, and when he is interviewed he speaks a variety of English that a Canadian recognizes.

I figure that ice hockey fans have their brain matter Osterized. At an NHL game there will be loud kids' music blaring right up to the moment that the puck is dropped for a face off. This is just in case the people in the seats let their attention stray toward a consideration of the news events of the day or the nuances of international economics. I am thinking that when hockey fans are at home watching videos of great hockey fistfights, they are also listening to some head banger heavy metal tracks by bands that play with their shirts off.

I don't know about fans of football, or as the people in the game call it, "foo'ball." Inasmuch as all the coaches and players and colour commentators speak in some rural southern palaver, I figure their tunes have to be shit-kickin' country and western stuff. Even in the Canadian Football League, the coaches and spectators say "DEE-fense," as if they were all from somewhere in the environs of Tuscaloosa.

So, the baseball fans I know feel superior to the followers of those other sports, and it strikes me that jazz aficionados feel similarly superior to the folks that listen to those inferior musics listed above. In fact, most of my baseball-breathing set are people who like jazz, and are as demanding in their recitation of data as are baseball nuts.

So I was not surprised when I found Nate Dorward's name while doing some Internet browsing recently. I met Mr. Dorward, along with his wife Jane at the big SABR convention in Toronto in 2005. Jane was the main organizer of the conference, and Nate was the city's voluble expert on baseball. What did my recent browsing turn up? Lots of interesting jazz reviews by Mr. Darwood, and the information that he runs a poetry magazine as well. This is not an amateur poetry magazine – it is a home for the best of the avant-garde.

Okay, I have noticed that a lot over the years. My baseball friends like jazz and poetry. I am also putting my money on Mexican food.

NAMES

There are a lot of silly things I shout from the stands when I am at a ball game. Here is one of them: when the PA announces a visiting player as, say, Ricardo Rodriguez, I shout "What kind of name is that for a baseball player?"

It helps that I am a visibly old coot.

Of course, if I look around major league rosters at the time of this writing, I find nine full time players named Rodriguez, nine named Gonzalez and ten named Ramirez. In minor league baseball you can't find a team without at least one of these names in the lineup. In fact I just took two teams at random and checked their rosters. The Round Rock Express, Houston's Triple-A team, employs Yordany Ramirez in the outfield. Seattle's High-A team, the High Desert Mavericks, has Juan Ramirez on the mound.

You just get used to having players whose names end in zed. I wonder whether the New Orleans Zephyrs have any? Yep. Carlos Martinez pitches for them. So does Carlos Vazquez. Andy Gonzalez plays shortstop and Gaby Sanchez is at first base. The Z's don't have any of those guys in the outfield, but Edwin Rodriguez is their manager.

[Open declaration: on the last team I played for in the Twilight League I was part of the double play combination with a guy we called Speedy Gonzales. His real name was Jose Rodriguez.]

113

I like having all these names buzzing around baseball, partly because I can speak and read Spanish a bit, and it's a really neat language to enunciate. When I was young I was so glad when Chico Carrasquel came up with the White Sox in 1950. When he left that team he was succeeded by the best name of all, Luis Aparicio. Since the fifties the White Sox have had a lot of good Latino shortstops, but none with as exciting a name as Luis Aparicio. Of course in 1956 almost everyone in US baseball pronounced both names wrong.

There are only really two problems with Spanish names. They aren't funny (Rusty Kunts) or allegorical (Matt Batts). Only rarely do they add to the fun-filled gathering of comical minor league handles, as when we were in Bellingham, Washington and saw a game that featured both Elgin Bobo, and Arquimedes Pozo. Wouldn't it have been wonderful if Luis Aparicio's parents had named him after the great mathematician?

Remember Vida Blue? Wasn't it a shame that he played for the Athletics instead of the Royals? Or maybe it was a wonderful daily event that he got dressed with a contradiction on the back of his shirt. In basketball Carlos Boozer played for a team in a Mormon state. Do you think that the Indians' owners ever thought of trading for Reggie Cleveland? On the other hand, they did trade away Allie Reynolds.

Here's another thing that I have noticed about names since they started that business of putting names on players' backs. It seems as if the skinny little shortstops from Venezuela and the Dominican Republic have such long names that they have to start up one sleeve and cross right over and down the other. But your average giant at first base? His name is Lum or May.

NATIONAL

Tonight the all-star game will be performed in a National League park, and I will sit in front of my normal television set for four hours while the American League wins for the 122nd year in a row. In the

American League there are players and teams that I like but I do not like the American League. It was so like the American League to opt for the designated hitter. I am a National League guy. My fantasy league uses players from the National League. We owners know that the squeeze play is a lot more exciting and gratifying than the strike-out of the big guy going for the three-run homer.

Yes, I will admit that Earle Weaver had the odds right, and that he had a heck of a winning percentage. But I am glad that the National League beat him three times out of four in the World Series. On another subject, I wish that the minor league teams in Vancouver had not been associated with American League bigs – Oakland, California, Baltimore, the White Sox, and now Toronto. One year we were the Triple-A affiliate of the Pittsburgh Pirates, and I was happy for a few months. But you take what you can get. Ask the fans in Kansas City.

I'm not a foo'ball fan, but I idly hope for the NFC in the so-called Super Bowl. I'm no longer a hockey fan, but I support any so-called "original six" team in any playoff. I like softball if it is fast-pitch, but sneer at the game called Slo-Pitch. If I were a weekend golfer I would never take a Mulligan or a gimme on a four-inch putt.

I decided to be a National League fan when I was a kid, before the invention of the DH or the Oakland A's. When I was a kid the American League would always win the All-star Game and the American League (aka Yankees) would always win the World Series. As the person who would read the Erle Stanley Gardner books but never watch the "Perry Mason" television series, I had to favour the Senior Circuit, if you see what I mean. In my world, NL fans read Joseph Conrad and AL fans read Stephen King. NL fans put mustard and relish on their hotdogs while AL fans put ketchup on theirs. NL fans listen to John Coltrane while AL fans listen to Kenny G.

When major league baseball came to Montreal I was so glad that the Expos were in the National League. After all, the Montreal Royals had been the Dodgers' Triple-A fount. When it was rumoured that the San Francisco Giants were going to move to Toronto, I loved the prospect of a neat rivalry. But then Organized Baseball, those creeps, put the kibosh on that deal, and when Toronto achieved major leaguedom it had to be in the American League. As a patriotic Canadian I still had to root for them to beat the Braves and the Phillies in the World Series, but I did it in secret (on one occasion in Arkansas).

And what about this? Remember back when the two leagues' umpires were quite different from one another? Remember when the American League home plate umpire wore that big mattress outside his jacket? Boy, that was goofy!

NOISE

First I'd like to say that when we went to a Hawks game at Memorial Stadium, I enjoyed the Noise in Boise.

Ta dum!

Okay, now that I have that off my chest I will not foist any more of that stuff on you, Boysie. My topic is not really noise, but the command to make some. Remember back in the day when live audiences at televised shows would be encouraged to clap their hands when the APPLAUSE sign was lit up? Then when live audiences were told to stay home, the television bozos created the laugh track. Any kid growing up through those times knew that the whole thing was fake.

At least baseball was real. Then they invented the JumboTron©. On this big shining capitalist marvel, if you can find some space between the advertisements for beer and trucks, you will often see the batting average of your shortstop. But when the game has settled in and you have the opportunity to think about out pitches and pinch hitters, some dolt hits a switch, and in big bright letters you see this on the screen: MAKE SOME NOISE. If you are in a multi-tiered major league stadium you might see this zooming around the park on the facing below the top deck: NOISE NOISE NOISE NOISE NOISE NOISE NOISE NOISE NOISE NOISE NOISE. Any baseball fan knows that this is where the game is falling into the hands of some people from a world that doesn't give a coon's poop for the game. If you are like me you keep preternaturally quiet during this moment. Or you make a very rude noise indeed.

The knuckle-draggers who light up those NOISE signs are also sometimes PA announcers. I feel patronized by one of these bozos at the beginning of every home game, when I hear him bellow, as the guys in white are taking the field: "here are *your* Vancouver Canadians." Oh, I get it! The guys in white are the home team! They come out onto the field first! They belong to *us*, the people in Vancouver who come to the game! Ah, I get it! Gee, I wonder when we are supposed to make some noise?

In the last year or two, this same loudmouth has been giving us new instructions for our demeanor during the playing of the national anthems. In Vancouver we get two of them, the US one all about bombs and rockets, and the Canadian one that excludes immigrants, women, and logic. In the last year or two the bozo on the PA has been telling us to stand and remove our hats. Well, I was in the Royal Canadian Air Force. We did not remove our hats for the National anthem. In fact we could not even salute without a hat on. The Yanks could. They are the people who take their hats off when the music comes. I wonder how long it will be until the bozo on the PA tells us to place out hats over our hearts.

At least we don't usually have guys with guns marching in from the outfield during the anthem, the way they do in Oklahoma City and Atlanta. Now wouldn't that be a bad time for the JumboTron© to order some NOISE?

NOSTALGIA

Baseball has always been a great game for nostalgia, but I seem to remember being more nostalgic in the old days. I still, though, look back fondly and with regret about a lot of things.

I miss going to the movies in October and hearing Mel Allen tell us what happened in the first two games of the World Series while we watched images of shadowed Yankee Stadium on the screen at the Oliver Theater. Of course we already knew who had won game six.

I miss being in the press box atop the rickety grandstand in Oliver and playing our old 78 RPM record of "Take Me out to the Ball Game" on the PA during the seventh inning stretch. I can't remember who sang the song, but whoever it was sang the part you usually don't hear: "Nelly Kelly loved baseball games/ Knew the players, knew all their names ...."

I miss baseball socks, a pair of white sanitaries, with stirrups over them, and the way you sit and fix them with your pants down. My fantasy team is called, you'll remember, the High Sox. The other night I saw the Boise Hawks play in Nat Bailey Stadium here in Vancouver. The Hawks were all wearing high socks, though no stirrups, and the hometown Canadians were wearing those sloppy pyjama pants hanging over their white spikes. I almost cheered for the visitors.

I miss the St. Louis Browns, the Washington Senators, the Boston Braves, the Philadelphia Athletics, the New York Giants, the Brooklyn Dodgers, the Seattle Rainiers, the Milwaukee Millers, the Oakland Oaks, the Newark Eagles, and the San Francisco Seals.

I miss my dad's office pool for the World Series. He was the chemistry teacher at our high school, and they had a beautiful complicated pool for each game. The tickets were probably a dime or something, but you might have Brooklyn winning 3–0 in the third game, or something. I guess having a fantasy team is an outgrowth of that kind of excitement.

I miss baseball on the radio. Up in the mountains of southern British Columbia I could tune in games from Seattle, Sacramento, San Diego and Salt Lake City. Later I enjoyed driving across Montana, say, at night, listening to a game from Billings. I wouldn't know the play-by-play guy and I wouldn't know any of the players, but I had to keep driving till the game was over.

I miss Maury Wills. During the 1960s he was the most exciting player in major league baseball. He put base stealing back in the game. In 1962, when he was the National League's MVP he got 208 hits and batted .299, but he stole 104 bases in 117 attempts. And get this: he came to the plate 759 times! He didn't do much in his forty-something games for the Expos in 1969, and the Expos' Tim Raines turned out to be a more proficient base stealer and hitter, but Maury Wills brought an excitement to the game that had faded away during the era of Harmon Killebrew and Eddie Matthews. In 1959 Willie Mays led the National League with 27 steals.

I miss Willie Mays.

NUMBERS

The other day I was wearing the white tee shirt that comprised my uniform for the last ball team I belonged to before I broke my hip and put an end to my career as a lightning-fast baserunner. On the front is our team name in script: Paperbacks. There is also an image of a guy leaping for a ball, holding out not a fielder's glove but an open book. On the back of the shirt is my number: 27.

It's my favourite number. My unlucky number is what you would get if you doubled my favourite number and subtracted two. I ain't going to spell it out for you. Recently I published a little poetry book in which I celebrate all the body parts of my sweetheart Jean. There are thirty-one pages, and on each page there are twenty-seven words, in three stanzas, each stanza made of three lines containing three words each.

When I was in my twenties my favourite hockey player wore number 27, but that is just hockey, not baseball. When I did a reading tour of the Northwest Territories his name was on my travel agency. When I became the first Parliamentary poet laureate by a bill that originated in the Senate, he was a senator. But still, he was hockey. I believe that 27 is really a baseball number. Three times three times three.

Three is an important number. When the New York Yankees decided to wear numbers on their uniforms in 1929, Earle Combs took number 1, Mark Koenig took number 2, and Babe Ruth, the strikeout king, took number 3. He was one of three New York outfielders. He played a game in which on a normal outing there are three outs to an inning. There are three strikes to an out if you go out without striking the ball fairly. Funny game, eh?

Nine is an important number. When I was a kid the most exciting hockey player wore number 9, but that was still just hockey. In baseball the best hitter ever wore number 9. Ted Williams hit number three in the Red Sox lineup, and that was what he was doing in 1941, when Joe DiMaggio was performing his record 56-game hitting streak. During that streak DiMaggio batted .408. During DiMaggio's streak Williams hit .417. I can't remember Joe's uniform number.

Rule 1.01 of the Complete Officials Rules tells us "Baseball is a game between two teams of nine players." Ted Williams's Red Sox used to play that game. They played, in most games, nine innings. Isn't nine a wonderful number? There are nine muses, aren't there? The music of the spheres is made by nine spheres. Golf, that game played in October by Chicago Cubs personnel, features a front nine and a back nine. Dante's great epic is divided into three parts, and in the first of these there are nine circles of hell, the ninth being that to which spectators who reach out for baseballs in play are consigned.

And if you are going to pitch a perfect game how many batters do you have to retire in succession? 3 times 9 equals 27.

O'BRIENS

When I was a rural schoolboy I used to write away for autographs from baseball players. In a sports magazine I'd read that you just write to Johnny Pesky, say, care of The Red Sox at Fenway Park. The best I ever got was an actual letter by Enos Slaughter, followed a week later by an autographed picture from him. I also wrote to a few hockey players, and once I wrote to a couple of basketball players, the O'Brien twins, Johnny and Eddie, when they were playing for Seattle University. They weren't tall but they were famous. Johnny broke the NCAA scoring record. They once led the Seattle University Chieftains to victory over the Harlem Globetrotters.

Then they became the double-play combination for the Pittsburgh Pirates. As far as I know they are the only twins to play for a MLB team except for the Shannons who played for a season for the Braves in 1915, and the Cansecos for less time than that at Oakland. Ossie Canseco was once busted for steroids but he never did get as big as his brother. As for Minnesota – Kirby Puckett looked as if he might have been two guys inside that shirt that proclaimed him Twins, but there have never been twin brothers on the Minnesota roster.

There have, of course, been lots of brothers in the bigs, from the Deans to the DiMaggios to the knuckleballing Neikros, but I wonder whether there has ever been such a brotherloving team as the Pittsburgh Pirates. Most celebrated were the Oklahoma brothers Paul (Big Poison) Waner and Lloyd (Little Poison) Waner. They both got to the Hall of Fame, and how many brothers are there in that building? They always said that the best hitter in their family was their sister Alma. Unfortunately, the Waners played in an era that excluded Black people and athletes of the female persuasion.

The 1909 Pirates boasted the pitchers Harry and Howie Camnitz. Howie was their ace, hurling 283 innings, and racking up 25 wins against 6 losses, with an exemplary 1.62 ERA. His kid brother Harry pitched only four innings, and got kind of rocked.

1921 was a relatively interesting year for the Pirates. Outfielder Carson Bigbee batted .323 for the Bucs, while his older brother Lyle pitched eight innings and finished the season with a 1.12 ERA. The Morrison brothers also played on that team, Johnny pitching 144 innings for a record of 9–7 with a 2.88 ERA, Phil pitching only two-thirds of an inning.

In 1948, the greatest year in the history of human civilization, Elmer and Johnny Riddle laboured mainly on the bench for the fourth place Pirates. In 1955 Pittsburgh had brothers all over the place. While Johnny and Eddie O'Brien were stationed at second base and center field, the Freese brothers, Gene and George were fighting it out to see who was the third baseman for the last place team. Nowadays at PNC Park the infield is held down at the corners by Adam LaRoche and Andy LaRoche. One night in June of 2009 they became the first Pirates brothers since the Waners to hit home runs in the same game. What team did they do this against? The Twins.

It seems as if the only Pirates team that didn't have any brothers playing for it was that powerhouse of 1979 that won the World Series with gold stars all over their hats. Remember their theme song? It was Sister Sledge's hit "We are Family." It seems that the four Sledge sisters were the best thing that had happened to the team since the two Waner brothers lost the World Series to the Yankees in 1927.

OKANAGAN

What killed semi-pro baseball all over the map was the infestation of television. When television was new to the Okanagan Valley, people who used to go out and watch the baseball game on Sunday afternoon stayed home and watched whatever the one or two television stations had to offer, old Bowery Boys movies, maybe.

That's what happened to the Okanagan Mainline Baseball League in the late fifties or early sixties. For the life of me, I can't understand why people would give up the excitement of the sunny afternoon at the park, the Summerland Macs in town with the amazing Kato brothers around the infield, to go home and pull the curtains and watch a little black and white game show. It just goes to show what happens when a new drug hits town. It would happen again later with video games and cell phones.

The Okanagan Mainline baseball league had two teams in Kamloops, and one each in Vernon, Kelowna, Summerland, Penticton, Oliver and Trail. In those days it was just normal to have eight teams in a league, because that was what happened in the Majors. Before the formation of the OMBL there was an outfit called the Okanagan League, with four teams in British Columbia (Vernon, Kelowna, Penticton and Oliver) and four in Washington (Omak, Brewster, Tonasket and either Chelan or Republic). I had mixed feelings when we went all Canadian.

There were a lot of Protestants in town who said that we shouldn't have ball games on Sundays, ball games you had to pay fifty cents to see. I sort of agreed with them, but I loved baseball so much that I was willing to step a little closer to Hell. I wasn't even averse to making a bit of money on the Sabbath. Sometimes I joined the boys chasing foul balls for the dimes you got for returning them. Later I roamed the stands and autos with bottles of pop for sale. Still later I got to the roof of the grandstand to keep score and make notes for stories in the *Chronicle*.

What the heck is Mainline, I wondered. I have it figured out now: it must be the CPR geography that passes through Kamloops. I generally didn't go on road trips to Kamloops or Trail, so that I had to make up stories on those games from the anecdotes I gathered from the players on Monday.

And now I remember that Princeton was in the league for a while. The ball players there had jobs working in the Princeton Brewery. That was the first beer I ever had, and once in a blue moon I have a sip of beer that reminds me of how good it tasted. Each bottle in the case of twelve was wrapped in a kind of grey asbestosy paper. Now when I drive to Oliver to see my family I pass the remains of the old Princeton baseball stadium. I think Princeton was in the league when Trail wasn't.

In the Okanagan Mainline Baseball League there was a lot of talk about "imports." These were US American ballplayers that would be brought to town and given a job so they could be paid for playing ball. Some years back when I was doing research for a novel set in Kamloops, I found out that the baseball teams around there were bringing in US American "imports" in 1889. I remember feeling a little ashamed that we went to the States to get good ballplayers.

But I wish I could go back and see a game in Tonasket on a hot dusty July Sunday afternoon – and have one of those US American soda pops you couldn't get back home.

OLDER

When I was a kid my heroes were of course older than I, which meant that my comic book heroes were older than I, and my baseball heroes were older than I, and so were all the other pro ball players, in every sport. Of course they were. As I entered my teenage years, the ballplayers were still older. I came around after Joe Nuxhall. During my twenties the ballplayers were mainly older than I.

So the habit of thought was instilled in my youthful baseball head.

When I was forty-five I still thought of the baseball players as older than I. I think that most of the time I still do. I look at some relief pitcher taking his ease in the bullpen and notice a few lines in his face and think, yep, that guy's getting up there. He doesn't look like a boy any more. And I am looking at him as a guy somewhat older than I.

Why is this? I have heard other baseball nuts tell me that they think of the major league ballplayers as older than they. When we go to see the Vancouver Canadians play the Yakima Bears in the short season Single-A Northwest League, we notice that most of them are around twenty years old or less, but if any one of them makes it to the Athletics or the Diamondbacks we see them as older guys.

Look at Mike Lowell at third for the Red Sox. He looks way older than I. Or Mariano Duncan, the closer for Satan's team. When he takes his hat off in the bullpen you can see a lot of the skin on his head, and the hair that *is* there is pretty white in places. Older guys. But I'd hate to tell you how many decades old I was when these guys were born. Mike Lowell, it just occured to me, is younger than my daughter – and she's still my little kid!

Well, there is a force of realism that makes itself known to one, and it sets up an argument with your habitual juniorism. One looks at old Mike Lowell diving to his right to prevent an extra-base hit, and says to oneself: okay I *used* to be able to do that. So as the decades have gone by one has learned to wish all good things to the older players in the game. In fact Brian Fawcett maintains that I actively draft the oldest guys I can get for my fantasy team, which I deny. Well, I *do* have Jamey Moyer as a spot starter.

OSCAR

I met Oscar Soule in Havana in 2008, and fell for him over the next two weeks, as we shared space in the hotel bar, in the air-conditioned Chinese bus and in baseball stadiums all over the west end of the island. Oscar once told a newspaper in Washington State that there might be someone who knows more about baseball than he does, but nobody enjoys it as much as he does. I believe him.

We'd be sitting with a crowd of 45,000 people in Havana's colossal Estadio Latinoamericana, where there are no visible concession stands, twenty-four hungry *norteamericanos* wondering where our next nosh was coming from – and there would be Oscar, sitting behind us, in an aisle seat, with a pork sandwich in one hand and a cheese sandwich in the other. The rest of us in the CubaBall trip had learned to expect this. If we were in José A. Huelga Stadium in Sancti Spiritus, and the only guy selling a bun with ham in it was ensconced in the 17th row just foul of the left field corner, Oscar Soule would find him. And while he was munching the sandwiches he would have a big smile to go along with his round cheeks and his white Hemingway beard.

He was sharp like that when he was a little kid in St. Louis. He would carry his autograph book to the barbershop of the hotel where the visiting baseball teams stayed, and snaffle autographs off Mickey Vernon and Johnny Lindell, Connie Mack and Joe Paige. But his most prized possession is the signature of Stan Musial. He's still a Cardinals fan if you're talking about the National League, but he moved to Olympia in 1971, to teach Environmental Science at The Evergreen College, and he has been a Mariners fan ever since they were founded in 1977.

In fact, Oscar was at their home opener, and he still goes to all their home openers, reserving 300 tickets up behind the plate, because his friends will be there. A couple carloads of us British Columbians drive down each year and give Oscar big hugs, trying not to get the mustard from his hotdogs on our jackets. That is so much fun, though it is usually kind of cold, and sometimes snowing outside.

In 2008, Oscar was named the Mariners' Fan of the Year, and threw out the first pitch. I wish I had been there. I'd like to have seen what he had in his other hand.

In Cuba we were impressed by Oscar's shopping. Rum. Cigars.

Baseball caps. The Cuban kids loved him, crowding around to see the hundreds of pictures he took with his digital camera. I took pictures of Oscar being surrounded by kids and tour mates. Unfortunately, before he could get home to the Northwest, thieves stole his camera, US border employees took just about everything else.

But they didn't get his smile. We get that as often as we can.

OUT

We have grown up with the terms that decorate baseball, and they seem normal enough to use in talking about other stuff. You don't get to second base with someone's daughter. In fact you might even strike out with her. Some of the ideas you hear come right out of left field. Even while you were just asking for a ballpark figure.

Sometimes I try to put myself in the place of a stranger from, say, Botswana, who is new to baseball lingo. Then I imagine someone explaining things to me. He says the pitch was outside. Outside what, I ask. Outside the strike zone. The next pitch comes inside. Inside the strike zone? No, that would be a strike. You mean the batter would strike the ball so that it soars out there where all that grass is? No, no, a strike is what happens when the pitch is not inside but in the strike zone, but the hitter misses, or doesn't try to hit it. What? I ask, the hitter does not hit?

Let me try something else, the baseball expert tells me. If the hitter hits, or strikes, no, if he bats the ball to the shortstop and the shortstop throws the ball to the first baseman before the batter, or runner now, I guess, gets to first base, the runner is out. You mean he is outside? No, I mean he is not safe. Safe from what? Um, I have never thought of that; safe from being out, I guess. Try me on something else, I say, in my Botswanian accent.

See that man out there? He is the center fielder, says the baseball expert, more confident now. Oh, and the man to his left is the left fielder? Well, no, the left fielder is to his right, and the man to his left is the right fielder. Uh huh, I say. Okay, don't give me any hints about those guys around the soil. The first baseman plays at third base? No, no, says my expert friend. Maybe I should explain the catcher first. Aren't they all catchers, I ask. Catchers and throwers? Okay, he says, forget the catcher, and I won't even bring up the shortstop.

What, I ask, is the purpose of that white line on the ground. Oh, that, he says, smiling now because he thinks that he has an easy one to explain. That is the foul line. Oh, I say, eager to meet his confidence with enthusiasm. That would be what we call the touch line in soccer. If the ball touches that line, play is stopped momentarily. His face looks a little sad. No, he says, if the batted ball falls on that line it is still in play. It is called fair. So the foul line is fair, I say, nodding my head. What about the yellow pole? Is that the fair pole? Uh, well, no, that's the foul pole, and if the batted ball hits that it is a home run. You get a home run on a foul ball?

Now my expert has taken off his baseball cap and is scratching the top of his head. I think I am going to have to give up, he says.

Oh no, I say. I was hoping that you could tell me this: if there are none out, with runners on first and second, and you are trying to sacrifice bunt but you pop it up in fair territory, is the infield fly rule in effect?

PACIFIC

Back in the day, the Pacific Coast League saw itself as something a notch above the International League and the American Association. There were ballplayers who had to think for a while before deciding whether to take up an invitation to the Big Leaguers or stay in the PCL. Lefty O'Doul was born in San Francisco, started a restaurant chain in San Francisco, and died in San Francisco. He started his baseball career as a pitcher with the San Francisco Seals, and after a few years was brought "up" to the American League. After he developed arm trouble the Red Sox let him go, so he came back to the Seals and became a power hitter. So the Bigs brought him back "up," where he did rather well, for instance in 1929, when he got 254 hits, to bat .398 with 32 homers and 122 runs batted in.

Later he became he best manager in the Pacific Coast League, and also got the redoubtable Tokyo Giants up and running. So Lefty is in the Hall of Fame, isn't he? Well, he was inducted into the Japanese baseball hall of fame in 2002. He was that good an ambassador. Too bad he wasn't good enough for Cooperstown. Okay, he won two batting championships with the Phillies and the Dodgers. His lifetime batting average was .349, fourth best ever in the Bigs. His 254 hits in a season is still a National League record. The trouble is that he spent a lot of years in San Francisco. His "minor league" lifetime batting average is .352. His last at bat was in the service of the Vancouver Mounties when he was 59 years old. It was a triple.

Joe Tinker (lifetime: AVG. 262, HR 31, OPS .661) is in Cooperstown. Lefty O'Doul is not. Despite his playing stats, his great managing history and his baseball ambassadorness, he was snubbed when he became eligible. I think that I may know why; at the end of his playing career and for much of his managing career, the Pacific Coast League refused to be termed Triple-A like the International League and the American Association. The league preferred the O classification, that letter standing for "Open." It was an era, what with transcontinental air travel and television, when there was a lot of talk about the PCL becoming the third major league. In fact a lot of people in offices in San Diego and Oakland said that it already was.

After all, teams in the PCL sometimes played 190 games a season out there in the nice climate. A lot of teams offered salaries equal to those a player might get in humid Cleveland or scorching St. Louis. Why would a manager like Lefty O'Doul want to work in Philadelphia or Washington when he could manage in San Francisco and Oakland?

Well, the panjandrums back east decided to put down those uppity west coasters, parachuting the Giants and Dodgers into California in 1958, eventually chasing the PCL teams out of those nice markets as well as San Diego, Anaheim, Oakland and Seattle. The PCL became Triple-A, and because Lefty O'Doul was so much identified with it, they froze him out of the Hall of Fame. You know, where Bowie Kuhn is.

PADRES

What is it about the San Diego Padres? When it comes to major league team caps in my collection, there are teams that I have more than one cap for. I have two different Milwaukee Brewers caps, for heaven's sake! I don't have a Tampa Bay cap because I have always held out for the black one with the TB *and* the ray. I don't have a Yankees cap for obvious reasons. I have all the rest, except for a Padres cap. Sometimes I wish I had that ugly brown and yellow one with the funny shape on the front. I have a decent minor league collection, including two different Tacoma caps and four different New Orleans ones. But I can truly say that I don't really know why I don't have San Diego Padres headwear.

Is it because I listened to San Diego Padres games on the radio when they were in the Pacific Coast League? Is it because every time I bought a package of bubble gum I always got a John Kruk baseball card? Is it because when expansion came I could not believe that San Diego could have a team in the National League instead of the American League, where places like Kansas City and Dallas belong?

I mean after all, I did once write a short story that featured some San Diego Padres along with some Minnesota Twins. After all, I was a big Tony Gwynne fan the same way I was a Rod Carew fan. As I mentioned at the ball game yesterday, I love that leadoff single. After all, I do have a Padre on my fantasy team, albeit an early reliefer.

Jean and I even highlighted San Diego on one of our famous baseball road trips. In 2004 we drove from the Niagara region to Vancouver by way of El Paso and Tucson. When you get to San Diego, I told Jean the number one driver, turn right. But before we did, we went to a game against the Rockies in the ridiculously magnificent Petco Park. Hey, maybe *that's* the problem – a home field named after a dog food! But the place is a wonder. We got there during its first season, and were impressed by the hundreds of volunteers, middle-aged women with big smiles and authentic pride in their building. Well, it's more like a small city than a building.

It's pretty corny, but most of the best things in baseball are. We sat in the porch in left field, and watched a Larry Walker line drive bang against the fence just in front of us. This sort of thing is the reason for driving the Interstate for weeks at a time. If it weren't for the military occupation, San Diego would even be an all right place to live. Once in the Eighties I spent a whole afternoon in a little pool-player Chicano bar in City Heights, forgetting that we were supposed to be on our way downtown.

I remember that I was wearing a Chicago Cubs cap at the time. I wish it had been a Padres cap, even a brown and yellow one.

PAIGE

I sometimes wonder whether Satchel Paige ever pitched against Suitcase Simpson. I do know this: I once saw Suitcase Simpson play in Mexico City, but I only almost believe that I saw Satchel Paige play, way back when I was a kid in Saskatchewan and my dad took me to see a barnstorming Negro team. But I was never in Saskatchewan until I took the train across it when I was joining the air force, and my father had not been in Saskatchewan since he crossed it to go to college in Manitoba more than a decade before I was born. A lot of stories about Satchel Paige are like this.

See, Satchel Paige is the most mythological player in baseball history, more mythological than Babe Ruth, more mythological, even, than Shoeless Joe Jackson or Dizzy Dean. He may have been the greatest ever pitcher in baseball, too.

Nobody knows how many games Satch won. Heck, nobody knows how many games he *pitched*. Sometimes he pitched two games a day. He pitched for the Birmingham Black Barons in 1927, while Babe Ruth was hitting sixty home runs and Gene Tunney came back from the "Long Count" to defeat Jack Dempsey. He pitched for the Kansas City Athletics in 1965, while the Houston Astros played their first season inside the Astrodome and Muhammad Ali knocked out Sonny Liston in Lewiston, Maine.

If you want to know what the United States was like in, say, 1942, meditate on the fact that Satchel Paige was the best pitcher in the country but he could not get into white restaurants in Kansas City. "The only change," he was to say, "is that baseball has turned Paige from a second-class citizen to a second-class immortal." A lot of people who collect quotations from Satchel Paige like to leave that one out, preferring the funny ones. Here is another one they leave out: "They said I was the greatest pitcher they ever saw. I couldn't understand why they couldn't give me no justice."

White America liked his windmill windup and his sky-high leg kick, the way they liked the droopy eyelids of Stepin Fetchit. "They [the sports writers] started talking about me like I wasn't even a real guy, like I was something out of a book." But if you were an African American living in Mobile, Satch's home town, you were clearly identified in one kind of book; in the city directory you had a lower case "c" placed after your name.

Even when the Cleveland Indians signed him on what was either his 42nd birthday or his 48th birthday in 1948, the greatest year in civilization, *The Sporting News*, the sports paper of record in the US, said that it was a stunt that demeaned baseball. Then in less than a half season, Paige proceeded to win six games, lose one and save one, while posting a 2.48 ERA, which was a very low number in those times. One of his starts brought out 78,382 fans, a Cleveland record. As a twelve-year-old in a little Canadian apple town, I loved all this. Even though the Indians defeated my beloved Red Sox in the playoff game, I loved Satch's season.

If there was one baseball player in the twentieth century that I wish I could have seen, it's Satchel Paige.

PELOTA

In the summer of 1964 we rented a house on Calle Beisbol in a southern barrio of Mexico City. Wasn't that one of one's dreams come true? It was ninety dollars a month, but I was willing to be gouged a little to get an address like that. It was a long but easy drive along the wonderful high speed city arteries to Foro Sol, where the famous Diablos Rojos, the best team in the Mexican League, played their home games. There I saw them defeat los Pericos de Puebla, whose outfielders stood on the warning track because Mexico City is more than 7,000 feet above sea level.

Harry "Suitcase" Simpson was one of those Red Devils, proving that he could still catch up to a fly ball at age 38. And there was Bobby Treviño, who four years later would stay long enough to get nine hits for the California Angels. And there under the unthinking cruelty of the *sol* was my vegetarian friend Sergio Mondragón, sniffing the deep-fried taco I had brought him, hoping that it was filled with *queso* rather than *seso*, the only alternative at the riotous concession stand.

It would take me forty years to get to another Mexican baseball game. Three days before Christmas of 2004 Jean and I went to Estadio Teodoro Mariscal to watch the Venados de Mazatlán host the Algodoneros de Guasave in a Pacific League contest. Did I say a "baseball game"? It was a festival. While Venados and Algodoneros were delivering wild pitches and errant throws down on the field, the twenty thousand revelers in the stands were singing, laughing, dancing, shouting, quaffing, gobbling, swaying, whistling, juggling, backflipping and generally having the time of their Sinaloan lives.

There were two big JumboTron screens. One showed the pitcher working up the nerve for another fastball. The other showed the bouncing breasts of the women in the crowd who were vying for the camera's attention with their own brand of *pelota*.

Unimaginable and unimaginably tempting food was being toted past one's nose all through the four and a half hours it took to play the game. Provocative *muchachas* bounce by and in a minute or two bounce by in the opposite direction. Two announcers, one female, shout into the PA mikes, and trumpet-crazy Mexican music blasts the nearby palm trees. People keep changing their seats, and whole families reconfigure the grandstand, hot prawns in one hand, lamb meatballs in the other.

The game drags on. Pitching coaches want to be noticed, so they walk to the mound every inning. When they make a pitching change, the reliever saunters in from deep center field, and then takes about a dozen warm-up pitches before facing his three or four batters.

Jean's eyes are sparkling. My saliva is on my chin.

This is *México*, everyone is telling us. We play the *beisbol* here. And we think you could use a *Bohemia Obscura*.

POEM

When I was the Parliamentary Poet Laureate of Canada I was asked by the Governor General whether I would write a poem for her to take to the president of Spain, and I didn't. A few Members of Parliament asked me for poems for some occasions too, and I didn't. But when Little League Canada asked me for a poem to print in the program for their annual tournament, I said sure.

Opening Day
– for George Stanley

On opening day
you can open your stance,
you can open a book,

take a good look, yeah,
take a liking, like
to a Viking.

Take a swing at a thing
like a sinker, ahuh,
be a thinker,

think of getting down to second,
take a second.

take a look.
take a lead-off,
read a book.

Rounding third, like a bird,
read the sign
from your coach,
your approach

to the plate,
isn't late,
isn't great,
but okay, okay, okay,

okay, you're safe,
safe at home

read a poem,
read *this* poem,

read about base,
read about ball,
read about baseball.

I mean don't delay it.
Get down and play it.

QUARRINGTON

Canadians are fond of pointing out the fact that basketball was invented by a Canadian, and a few even know that the first ever NBA game was played in Toronto. The first university team to play football was McGill, in 1864, five years before the famous game at Rutgers. There was a lot of baseball being played in Ontario before Abner Doubleday invented the game in upstate New York. But Canadians have never claimed to have invented baseball. Baseball was played in England while the Canadian aboriginal people were playing their stick-and-ball game later called Lacrosse by the European immigrants.

A lot of these things would come as surprises to a lot of US Americans, because (1) they believe that they invented pretty well anything, and (2) they are not much interested in what goes on in other countries. So, it is unlikely that there would be a Canadian story in an anthology of baseball fiction published in, say, New York or Minneapolis, but if there was, the reader would just consider the writer to be a US American. Canadians, on the other hand, would be jumping up and down and loudly describing the author's birthplace. They would do that with Saul Bellow, for example, if he would get off his duff and write a baseball fiction, the way a good Jewish-American novelist is supposed to do. You know the books I'm talking about.

When I edited a collection of baseball fiction I included writers from Japan and Nicaragua as well as the USA and Canada. The Nicaraguan author was an official in the Sandinista government, so he was probably not read all that much in Ohio. The Canadians included the usual suspects, including Mordecai Richler and W.P. Kinsella, both of whom are often assumed to be US Americans by readers south of Canada.

But my anthology did not include anything by Paul Quarrington. What a dunce I was in the late eighties when I was putting *Taking the Field* together! In the early eighties Quarrington had published his second novel, *Home Game*. Quarrington would produce a lot of wonderful novels over the next two and a half decades, including *Civilization*, which, though it is mainly about the riotous early days of Hollywood flickers, has some brilliantly funny baseball stuff in it.

I have often said that the 80-page baseball game in Philip Roth's *The Great American Novel* was the funniest 80-page description of a baseball game in the canon. But along comes Paul Quarrington's 80-page description of a baseball game in *Home Game*. The former offers an opposition team made up of people in a loony bin. The latter gives us a home team made up of circus freaks and carnival geeks. I'd say we'll get extra innings.

Then ten years later, in *Civilization*, the opposing pitcher is Charlie Chaplin, whose delivery sometimes includes pratfalls off the mound.

If you are a literary baseball fan in the lower forty-eight, do your best to locate Quarrington's books. He is way up there in baseball fiction, and he is for sure in my rotation when it comes to Canadian novelists.

QUÉBEC

I didn't have the poutine at *Stade Municipal*, because I figured that ballpark poutine is probably to poutine as ballpark nachos are to nachos. It was August 19, 2005, and according to our tickets, *les Capitales de Québec* were playing the Bangor Lumberjacks. However, according to our several senses, which were operating in at least two languages, the visiting team that *les Capitales* defeated 12–5 was the Grays, a team that plays only road games.

In fact, now that I come to think of it, I wish that I had been able to acquire a Grays cap. Its logo was a little strip of highway, complete with dotted centre line. But at the time I was mesmerized by the beautiful *Capitales* hat, which is still the best one in my collection, though I am very fond of the light blue Portland Beavers cap I have acquired more recently.

You know that you are in another country when you sit in the mezzanine of *Stade Municipal*, just as you do in Mazatlán or Bologna. Not only are there really people consuming poutine and other colorful local fare, but you are reminded that 98% of Quebeckers like to smoke cigarettes every minute of their waking lives, preferable two cigarettes at a time. I don't know another ballpark in which you can puff cancer, but culture is culture. Oh, and beer. This is also the only ballpark I know of in which fans can buy two pints of beer each in the top of the ninth inning.

Les Capitales play in what most people call the CanAm League, but which calls itself The Canadian-American Association of Professional Baseball. It's an independent league that used to include the North Shore Spirit of Lynn, Massachusetts, a team we missed seeing for the pathetic reason I have told you about. A lot of the people in the city of Québec will tell you that they think the league should be the Québec-US Association, but then what is in a name? Are there any non-US teams in the International League this year? Are there any Pacific coast cities in the PCL?

Ballplayers in independent leagues like the CanAm come in all sizes and sorts. There are those who think they might rack up some newsworthy statistics and get a tryout with a MLB team. There are those who just like playing baseball and getting a few dollars for it, those like Pete Rose Junior who were in what their owners call "organized baseball" and are now just a step sideways from Single-A. Then there are guys such as Eric Gagne, who was born in Montréal, won the Cy Young Award with the Dodgers in 2003, and in 2009 was hurling for *les Capitales de Québec*. There's a drawing card.

Speaking of cards, there was another thing I got at *Stade Municipal* – a pack of player cards. Someone was handing them out free. They were entirely in French with a few stats and a story about coming to Jesus as a personal saviour. Bill Mueller, for example, was *"Champion des frappeurs de 2003 dans la ligue américaine,"* and says of his experience of Jesus that *"Il m'apporte beaucoup plus de satisfaction que le baseball."* You can find out more at www.monhistoire.ca.

The official motto of *les Capitales* is *"La Victoire est en Nous!"* I wouldn't be at all surprised if some of the people who speak these words are thinking of something that goes beyond baseball.

Wait a minute. Did I just write the words "goes beyond baseball"? Wash out my mouth with poutine!

QUEENS

One winter, because of a reported blizzard around Toronto, we had to spend New Year's Eve in a crummy hotel or motel or maybe stockyard in Queen's, a place where there was puke on the elevator floor. On the way there we saw desolate Shea Stadium, a sad round thing in the swirling cold. Overhead, passenger jets struggled into the sky. Never come back here – that's the message I was getting.

But I did. In late September of 2008 we went to the second last game played at Shea Stadium, sitting in the uncovered upper deck on a day of blue sky and 90 US degrees, and a humidity that an octopus could have swum in. We were hoping to see the Mets lose, of course, because that's what they did in the late part of the season in the new millennium, and it was such fun to listen to the comic badmouthing from their fans. We were lucky enough to move to a spot high behind the plate for the late innings, to be surrounded by ironic New Yorkers and their dire predictions.

From our vantage we could see the half-built new stadium that would be named after a bank. I was glad to be in this dump before they tore it down. It was perhaps the ugliest of all those round multi-sport heaps by which the National League was plagued between 1964 and 1970. Shea had an unfortunate odor, narrow concourse, uncomfortable narrow seats, and despicable toilets.

There were two pleasures besides the ironic fans. You could try to identify the passenger jets that roared a few hundred feet above the park. And the Atlanta Braves came from behind in the ninth inning to win 7–4. What I had heard for years proved to be true: Mets fans are smart, funny, generous and likewise in just about every other way the opposite of their counterpoints who support that other team with the letters N and Y on their hats.

And here is an observation that may or may not seem unlikely given all that: I have never been in a ballpark in which such a high percentage of the fans in wearing team caps and shirts. As for the shirts – I think that seventy percent of them had the name Wright on the back.

Jean came away from the home of Casey and Doc and Pedro with a new sunburn to add to her collection, and I was filled with gratitude to her for arranging this visit to Queens. I knew that she had purchased tickets to watch that team in the Bronx, and I knew that I could forgive her that after this historic trip to Flushing Meadows.

QUISENBERRY

If you are a baseball fan like me you like lefthanders, flakes, guys in glasses, bunters, knuckleballers, Australians, poets and place-hitters. You aren't all that fond of tattoo guys, monsters that strike out, Yankees, spitters, prayer-group leaders and cliché kings. So you liked Dom DiMaggio, Rod Carew and Jimmy Piersall. And you liked Dan Quisenberry.

I don't remember whether I ever saw Quiz pitch. The chances are good that I did, because there was a time when it didn't matter where I was seeing a Major League Baseball game, the visiting team was nearly always the Kansas City Royals. Even the interleague games I saw had KC in the visitors' dugout. So I probably saw the mustachioed righthander.

But it was not the seeing of Quiz that made an impression; it was hearing about something he said. There are certain baseball gents who were quoted a lot – Satchel Paige, Casey Stengel, Yogi Berra, Dizzy Dean. Add Dan Quisenberry. They even gave a name to his *mots*: Quisenberries.

It is not that Quiz was a comic journeyman – far from it. He led the American League in saves five times, the first pitcher to do that, and when he retired he was sixth lifetime, with 244 saves. He twice ended a season with an ERA under 2.00, and his lifetime mark was 2.76. His submarine delivery did not offer blazing fastballs, but it was deucedly hard to hit. He had a quickie that fell earthward hard in its last few feet, leading accusations that he was somehow medicating the ball.

He had some choice remarks about that famous sinker. "Natural grass," he said, which Kaufmann Stadium did not have until 1995, seven years after he left the Royals, "is a wonderful thing for little bugs and sinkerball pitchers." But what happens, he was asked by *Sports Illustrated* in 1980, if the sinker isn't working quite right? "The batter still hits a grounder," he replied. "But in this case the first bounce is 360 feet away."

I suppose you remember my mentioning poets in the list I gave you up there. The much-travelled pitcher Miguel Batista has published a book of poems entitled *Sentimientos en blanco y negro* and two novels, all of which have sold well in the Dominican Republic. While other players are listening to rap music and reading hunting magazines, he is reading psychology and philosophy. Why not? His middle name is Descartes.

Dan Quisenberry didn't publish his poetry until after his retirement. In 1995 he published some poems in journals and a chapbook entitled *Down and In*, and two years later started to gather them for a book. Just while he was doing that, he was diagnosed with a brain tumour. In 1998 his book *On Days Like This* was published. It was part of a big Quisenberry celebration held at Kaufmann Stadium and shown all over on television. At the end of the regular season, Dan Quisenberry died.

His main nickname was Quiz, of course. But they also called him The Australian because of his "down under" pitch delivery.

QUIZ

1. In 1950, how many MLB teams had nicknames that began with the last letter of their city's name?
2. With runners at first and second, and none out, your pitcher (you are smart enough to be a National Leaguer) bunts, but the ball pops up. The trouble is that their pitcher drops the ball, then picks it up and throws out the runner going to first, then their third baseman throws to second and gets the runner who was heading there. What does the umpire say?
3. In 1950, how many MLB teams had a colour in their names?
4. Who is the most reviled baseball player ever to have been born in the United Kingdom?
5. Who was the losing pitcher in the first World Series game?
6. Identify the writer of this: "And it was not very wonderful that Catherine, who had by nature nothing heroic about her, should prefer cricket, base ball, riding on horseback, and running about the country at the age of fourteen, to books."
7. What was the lifetime batting average of the Alou family? Which one had the highest average?
8. If the lights suddenly go out while your base runner is attempting to steal second, and come on again while he is standing on that bag, what does the umpire say?

9 Here's an easy one. The Phillies have white home uniforms with red pinstripes. Why are the i's in their name dotted with blue stars?

10 In the 1909 World Series, Ty Cobb was on first base and shouted to Honus Wagner, "I'm coming down on the next pitch, Krauthead!" What was the Pirate shortstop's reply?

11 "Left-handers have more enthusiasm for life. They sleep on the wrong side of the bed and their head gets more stagnant on that side." In your own words, tell us what Casey Stengel was saying here.

12 Which four movie actors have played both a baseball player and Wyatt Earp? Of all the actors who played Wyatt Earp, who did Wyatt Earp like?

13 If Early Wynne's mother had crowded the plate, would he have thrown at her?

14 In Feller's pickoff play in the first game of the 1948 World Series, how much was Phil Masi out by?

15 Who was the potential tying run on second when Casey (sorry to spoil it for you if you didn't know this) struck out?

RADIO

While I was walking around in San Francisco during the summer of 1962, I would hear Russ Hodges doing play-by-play out the windows of all the apartments and stores and streetcars. The great era of the transistor radio had arrived. Here is what I heard people asking each other all over North Beach and the Market District: "What's the score?" Or often: "What did McCovey do?"

Boy, I miss baseball radio. I know, I know, if you are one of those lucky people who live in major league cities, you still get to listen to your team lose another game to the Angels in late innings. But I live in a Low-A town, and while I think that there might be a few games on the dial here, I sure don't hear them at the barber shop.

This is another old fart telling you about how things were better in the old days. I can go into a bar anywhere in town and see twenty television sets high on the walls, and you know what's on those television sets? If you are lucky it is football or tennis. More likely it is six guys in sunglasses and stupid hats playing poker, or it is one of those tattoo things the gangsters like – ultimate banging or mixed muscular arts or something, two guys with buzz cuts wrapping their legs around each other and poking faces.

Television is okay for baseball, especially if it is accompanied by one of those dear old voices such as Vin Scully, who has been announcing the Dodgers since his first appearance on crystal sets when the Brooklyn team was called the Robins. He is the opposite of the amateurs that broadcast the Toronto Blue Jays games. They watch a ground out to the shortstop and then tell you that the batter grounded out to the shortstop. Vin Scully has a voice like buttered yams to start with, and he tells you interesting stuff that you would not know by glomming the infield.

But radio was way better than television for baseball. I didn't much like those "recreated" games called by a guy in a radio studio back home, using a pencil to sound like a bat employed by some Sacramento Solon on the road in San Diego. But I did listen to them. My favourite announcer was Leo Lassen, who croaked out the Seattle Rainiers games from KOL to all us kids snuggled beside radios between the mountains in Oregon, Washington and BC. We can now go to the Internet and listen to his recorded voice following the arc of a long fly ball: "back ... back ... back ..." he would rasp, and then matter-of-factly tell us whether it was an out or a homer.

Speaking of nostalgia: I don't know how often I drove a hundred miles farther on some night time trip just so I could hear the final out in the Billings-Great Falls game. Can I remember the score now? Of course not. But I remember the little glow put out by that radio in the middle of the dash.

RAMAZZOTTI

When I was in junior high there was a Cubs second baseman named Bob Ramazzotti, and I thought wow, he must be tough. I wouldn't want to get in *his* way. Ever since, I have thought of his name as a good example of toughness. Not till now did I look up his record, and I was a little taken aback. The most games he got into in a season were 1951's 73, and his lifetime batting average was .230. Still, he makes it as second baseman in my team of all-time tough-sounding names.

Who could argue with my choice of catcher? Matt Batts. He was from the same era as Ramazzotti, and he too was a part time player, but in his best year he got six home runs for the Cincinnati Reds. You could say that his name was made for baseball, but then Barry Foote was a baseball player too. Still, pretty tough-sounding.

I always thought that Kluszewski sounded pretty tough, maybe even dumb mean. I know that Ted was the first guy to tear off his jersey sleeves, creating a style that the Reds and Pirates and A's would adopt a few years later. From the same era as Ramazzotti and Batts, he was a bona fide slugger, and he weighed 225 pounds. He is my first baseman.

Hank Sauer is from that time too (was the postwar era a time for tough guys?), and he's one of my outfielders. It happens that he was kind of tough-looking, and if a guy that looks like that is also sour, you have to be a little intimidated. I'm tempted to add Hank Bauer to my outfield, but he was a Yankee, and who's afraid of a Yankee?

My starting righthander is Bill Stoneman. Come on, think of it. You are up to bat and what is he throwing up there? His name isn't Baseballman, is it? You still aren't impressed? He pitched two no-hitters as an Expo! Oh, and if you survive him, my righthanded reliefer is Eric Plunk. My lefthanded reliever pitched in eleven games for the 1914 Indians. His name is doubly threatening: Harley Dillinger.

And while I am at it, I think I will pick Bob Dillinger as my third baseman. I remember liking him a lot. Like a lot of my regulars, his short career started right after World War II. He wound up hitting .206 for his career, but started late because he was busy scaring the Axis powers till VJ Day. In 1948, the greatest year in human history, he led the American League in hits with 207. He also led the league in stolen bases three years in a row. He went to the Pacific Coast League for his last four seasons, leading that loop with a .366 batting average in 1953. He was the scariest ballplayer in eyeglasses.

I have a guy named Flash Archdeacon in my outfield. I guess that if you are not a religious type you won't be all that scared. He's a mystery more mysterious than Bob Dillinger. He had a .333 career average, but his career consisted of 384 at bats for the 1923–25 White Sox, with 288 of those coming in the 1924 season. I figure that if his name were High School Principal instead of Archdeacon, he might spread more fear.

To round out my outfield I was going to go with Bob Skinner, figuring that the implications ought to warn anyone away who was considering taking the extra base. But then I found out about a guy that put in a few innings for the Yankees and Red Sox in the early twenties: Elisha Harrison Camp Skinner. Okay, he did wear a uniform we all admire and detest, but come on – that first name cinches the fear factor for me, especially for spring training, eh?

Now to fill my lineup I need a shortstop, of course, and it won't be anyone named Peewee or Robin. After a lot of consideration, and with some nervousness about reader response, I have settled on Jack Glasscock. He was always the league-leading shortstop in the barehands, pebbly ground era, and always among the offensive pacesetters as well. If you feel that you are not in agreement that his surname is somehow scary, consider this: his given moniker is John Wesley Glasscock. John Wesley Hardin, the meanest man in Texas, was born four years before Jack, and instead of grabbing grounders he killed over forty men in cold blood. *That's* scary, at least.

RECORDS

I don't mean hitting in 56 games in a row, or pitching 507 wins. I mean 78s or 33⅓s or LPS or tapes or CDs. What we used to call records, which we would purchase in what used to be called record stores. Baseball did not do as well in popular music as it did in the movies. If William Bendix and Ronald Reagan gave us the lowest scores in cinema, they still finished ahead of all the recording "artists."

A typical effort might be "I Love Mickey" by Teresa Brewer and Mickey Mantle. This was a 45 issued by the Coral label in 1956. She would sing, "I love Mickey," and he would ask, "Mickey Who?" and she would offer a description of his ability, until the last time he asks her who, and she says, "Mickey You." Well. Teresa and the Mick got their photo on the cover of *Rock and Roll Songs* magazine, wherein one can see that the diminutive songstress did not know how to hold a baseball bat.

Mickey wasn't finished there. Two years later he had his picture (in which he holds a baseball bat with expertise) on the cover of an LP issued by RCA, entitled *My Favorite Hits/ Mickey Mantle*. On the back of the record jacket he is quoted as saying that next to baseball he was most interested in popular music. What are his favorite hits? They run from Artie Shaw's "Begin the Beguine" to "The Last Roundup" by the Sons of the Pioneers. On the jacket someone admits that the idea originated with someone at *Sports Illustrated*.

It seems as if Mickey Mantle is the subject of half the songs ever recorded about baseball. One that most of you will know is a song about the three really good center fielders who plied their trade in New York in the fifties – Willie Mays, Duke Snider, and ol' Mick. This is a ditty titled "Willie, Mickey and the Duke," as rendered by one Terry Cashman (and no, I don't know whether he was any relation) for Lifesong Records. It came out in 1981 – I suppose the hope was that it would make up for the baseball strike. You will remember some of its excruciating lyrics: "The Scooter, the Barber and the Newc, / They knew them all from Boston to Dubuque. / Especially Willie, Mickey, and the Duke."

It's not my fault.

I may have mentioned that the first major league game I saw took place between the Red Sox and Detroit at Tiger Stadium in 1967. It was the first game in a double header, and I wanted to see the second game, but my friend Greg Curnoe the lacrosse fan wanted to see the rest of Detroit. A couple years later, having come to realize that I loved the Red Sox, and that I had never seen a MLB game before, Greg gave me a present.

It was an LP from Capitol Records, titled *Denny McLain at the Organ*. Yeah. It was Denny's first album, and on the back of the jacket he is quoted as saying, "When it's all said and done some day in the future, I hope they will remember Denny McLain as an outstanding professional musician." On the front of the album is a phony picture of McLain pitching without a pitcher's rubber, in front of some cheesy little stands in some suburb. He would go on to make a second album concocted from Las Vegas appearances.

Denny knows a lot about records. He was the first pitcher to get the MVP and the Cy Young in the same year, the last pitcher to get thirty wins in a season, this for Detroit in 1968. He put out two organ records, as we have seen, and has a pretty hefty record as a recidivist behind various iron bars. And here is a rounding-out for Greg Curnoe: after his organized baseball career came to a druggy close, he joined the London (Ont.) Majors of the Intercounty League, pitching a little, catching, playing first base, etc. Maybe he played a little organ. You ought to hear him doing "By the time I get to Phoenix."

ROAD

At the time of this writing, my sweetheart Jean and I are preparing for this summer's road trip. Well, to be honest, Jean is doing the preparing, as usual, and I am doing more and more anticipating. I will get to add a new state to my life collection (Utah), and if things work out properly – that is, if they have my size – add the Casper Ghosts to my cap collection.

When I was a young fan I always dreamt of going on the road, visiting ballparks all over the continent, yucking it up with the locals and seeing what their beer was like. I think that all baseball fans have that dream or something like it. I know a guy my age who collects major league ballparks. I have been trying to persuade him to add the minors and the independents. I put the dream off for a long time, but it came true after I retired from my professoring job and lucked out with my sweetheart Jean.

I mean she organizes the route the way she organizes everything, with a determination and seeming ease that leave me open-jawed. If you run across my book *Baseball Love*, you will see a record of our first big road trip that took us from Vancouver to Buffalo by way of Boise and Pittsburgh. We have travelled a lot of roads since, passing through Tucson, Eugene, Cincinnati and Oklahoma City, for examples. So far our trips have got us seats at ballparks in five countries plus whatever Texas is.

But these road trips are not just about baseball, though baseball is the directional finder. We also check the former abodes of writers such as Ezra Pound, Ernest Hemingway and Sinclair Lewis. We suss out Mexican restaurants. Perhaps most important – we get to go to the great art museums plunked down in formerly successful US cities by wealthy donors. The Albright-Knox in Buffalo, the Cleveland Museum of Art, the Detroit Institute of Arts. We were lucky enough to visit the famously free Saint Louis Art Museum in 1904, the centenary of its opening during the World's Fair you hear so much about. We arrived at the amazing Toledo Museum of Art about a half hour before closing time. I didn't get past the big Matisse ceramics at the entrance. On the other hand there was Phoenix. Twice before I had tried to visit the Phoenix Art Museum, forgetting that it was Monday. At last we got there on an open day, and found it to be one of the least interesting big museums on the continent – unless you are fond of horse pictures.

But of course, the name of the game is baseball. When you see a game on television now, it somehow means more if you have been in the building in which it's being contested. And then, of course, there is memory, something you always encounter at SABR meetings and any other collection of old farts in old team jackets. Remember the way the last twenty feet of the left field foul line runs uphill in Bellingham? Remember how close home plate is to the screen in Visalia? Remember the people bringing folding money to stick in the screen for home run hitters in Midland?

Oh lord! Remember the sixth inning fish-toss in Missoula?

The New York World's Fair of 1939 took as its theme the World of Tomorrow. Its most famous image, the one that would appear on countless posters, on US postage stamps, in magazines all over the world and on the shoulders of all three New York major league baseball uniforms, was a representation of two buildings, the Trylon and the Perisphere. The first was a pointy tower and the second was a huge ball at its base.

That pairing has been repeated many times in more recent architecture and design. If you take in a home game of the Toronto Blue Jays now, you will be seated inside a big sphere that is situated at the foot of a high pointy thing called the CN Tower. The big sphere, when it was opened in 1989, was called the SkyDome. So its name as well as its shape was stolen, in this case from the arena at Northern Arizona University in Flagstaff.

The one in Toronto got that name as the result of a contest, the voters eager to point out that the stadium had the first mechanically retractable roof in sports. I was there one day when it was raining with the roof open, and as soon as the rain stopped, they closed the roof. Unsure on the concept, I thought. But the people in Toronto were pretty chirpy, because they had arrived in the American League the same year that the Seattle Mariners got there, and everyone knew that Seattle's Kingdome was a big ugly pinball machine.

But now Seattle has a new ballpark named after some insurance company, and it is a lot better than Toronto's in several ways. It has a retractable roof too, but when you are under it you can still see (and hear) outside. Thus you can have real grass. The Rogers Centre, as the Toronto dome is now called because a millionaire wanted his name on it, still uses artificial turf. Until 2008 Toronto's Triple-A affiliate was in Syracuse, where artificial turf was installed to give Blue Jay prospects some experience on that dreck. Essentially, the Rogers Centre, where football is also played, is like one of those erstwhile dreadful round things they used to play ball in in Pittsburgh and Cincinnati with a roof added.

Here's another way Seattle's stadium is better than Toronto's. In Toronto the slope of the tiers is so gradual that if you are in the fifteenth row you are a kilometer or two from the field. In Seattle the tiers are so steep that your feet are behind someone's head, and you are right up close to the action.

If you want to know how hip they are about baseball in Toronto, dig this. I was at a game in which a visiting slugger poled a fly ball into the seats in left. A fan pegged the ball back onto the plastic ground, imitating a Cubs follower. The PA announcer instructed the crowd that objects should not be thrown onto the field. Typical. Or how about this? In the top of the ninth some kids trooped down and took some first-row seats that had been abandoned by the businessmen who had sat there doing business. The ushers came down – in the ninth inning! – and chased them back upstairs. Toronto.

Oh, and one more thing. If you are sitting at home watching the game, you will probably want to turn off the sound. The Toronto Blue Jays have the worst announcers in all of organized baseball.

SEATTLE

The Seattle Mariners and the Toronto Blue Jays entered the American League in 1977, and when thousands of people from British Columbia jammed the Kingdome for any visit by the Jays, baseball people in Seattle were puzzled. How come Vancouverites cheered for the Jays rather than the Mariners? Seattle is only 120 miles down the I-5 from Vancouver, while Toronto is 3,365 kilometers away. The US Americans just didn't get it. Well, a lot of US tourists in Vancouver are surprised to see that we have our own flag up here.

Still, Seattle has always had a certain spot in my imagination, or at least in my fancy. Just as Torontonians watch Buffalo television stations, and people in my home town of Oliver, Wine Capital of Canada watch Spokane stations, so in Vancouver we have always watched US network shows on KING-TV and KIRO-TV and KOMO-TV. Before that, even back in Oliver, I used to listen to the radio stations that gave birth to these television outlets. So most of the baseball games I heard on the radio were played by the Seattle Rainiers of the PCL and announced by Leo Lassen on KOL. I was so lucky. Anyone who remembers listening to Leo do a ballgame, and he did them for three decades, will tell you that no one ever did them better. I miss him especially when I watch a Toronto Blue Jays game with the sound on.

When Leo saw a notoriously slow-of-foot power hitter make it to second base, he would say, "He's into second standing up, piano and all."

We go to opening day at Safeco Field in Seattle every year now, but I was one of the few ball fans who never denigrated the Kingdome. It took baseball people many years and several civic votes to get that concrete dome built, but it was cheap. For the price of Montreal's Olympic Stadium, Canadians could have built twenty Kingdomes across their country. Kamloops would have got one! Outfield seats were $2 at the Kingdome, but I would usually change my sitting place every inning or two, see the game from as many places as possible. Once down the left field foul line I said to 37-year old Gary Matthews, who was spending his only half-season in the American League, "Hey, didn't you used to be Gary Matthews?" He smiled and replied, "You got that right."

I *would* be a Mariners fan if I hadn't become a Red Sox fan when I was young and impressionable. I *do* wish them well in the American League West. And if the Sox can't be there, I wish that Seattle could be in the World Series, and if they were in the World Series against the Mets I would cheer for them. And I *do* want Ichiro Suzuki to win the batting championship every year.

And here is one more thing: Seattle is the nicest city in the United States.

SHORTSTOP

Every major leaguer who played Little League ball or its equivalent was a pitcher some days and a shortstop the rest of the time. All gung-ho kids want to play short. My kid brother was born late enough to get into Little League, and he was a pitcher and a shortstop. He doesn't follow baseball at all now. It just goes to show.

In San Pedro de Macoris, a city created by Cuban refugees on the coast of the Dominican Republic, baseball players and poets are the chief products. All the baseball players are shortstops. In fact the city is often called "The Cradle of Shortstops." Every team of young ballplayers there is made up of nine shortstops. Often when they get to the major leagues, and an amazing number do, they have to play other positions and do pretty well. Take for examples former shortstops such as George Bell, Sammy Sosa and Mariano Duncan.

If you can't run very fast but you can really scamper, chances are you could be a shortstop. This certainly applied to me during the few years when I was a shortstop – for the Granville Grange Zephyrs in the Kosmic League early in the 1970s. I also had a paper arm but really fast hands, a combination better suited for a second baseman, which I was by birth. Oh, but I loved playing shortstop in my late thirties! My Kosmic nickname was "The Whip." If I have told you this on another occasion, so be it.

Around that time a bunch of us ballplaying poet heroes were habitués of Section 9 at Nat Bailey Stadium, where our main ambition was to make taunts that could be heard by opposition players from, say, Spokane and Portland. But we also liked to cheer our Canadians' shortstop. In all of baseball, and especially in Vancouver, the shortstop happens usually to bear a Spanish name. So naturally, we always addressed our shortstop as "Wally."

"Nice throw, Wally!" we would holler.

One of these Latinos was Ed Romero, a Puerto Rican shortstop with the full name of Edgardo Ralph (Rivera) Romero. He got the gears from Section 9 for two Triple-A years, 1979 and 1980. Four years later I was sitting in Municipal Stadium in Cleveland, along with 7,000 other true fans, watching the Indians struggle against the Milwaukee Brewers. Imagine the Milwaukee shortstop's surprise when he heard my ungentle voice filling that huge cavern by Lake Erie: "Hey, nice throw, Wally!" Turned his head, I'll tell you.

After years and years of Iberian names, the Canadians got a shortstop with a nice white bread moniker. It might have been Dale Sveum, who usually played third. We had already nicknamed him "Mr.

Colour," but when he shifted over to short, Section 9 greeted him this way: "Let's get that double play, Jesús!"

Oh, speaking of names – I can't leave here without mentioning my favourite big league shortstop name of, as they say, all time. I'm talking about Yats Wuestling, who played for the Cards in 1929 and 1930, when guys were pounding home runs. Yats never got one, and in fact retired with a lifetime average under the Mendoza line. But even Nomar Garciaparra could not touch him for name.

SOX

By now you will know that I am a life-long Boston Red Sox fan. Of course I have in all that time assumed that naming a team after the colour of their socks is a good and normal idea. It doesn't seem to happen all that often in other sports, though. There is a soccer team called the Vancouver Whitecaps, but they are named after a windy day's effect on the nearby ocean. Soccer players do not wear caps all that much. There is a hockey team called the Columbus Blue Jackets, but just as soccer players do not wear caps, so hockey players do not wear jackets. Not in Ohio. Not in Quebec.

In basketball there are the New Jersey – no, forget it.

Anyway, we know that the full name of the Cincinnati team is the Red Stockings. And that is what they wear, or so we assume in this hiphoppy era in which you can't see most of the ballplayers' hosiery. My fantasy team is called the High Sox, in protest. If I am at, say, Spring Mobile Ballpark in Salt Lake City, and the Las Vegas 51s are in town, I will cheer for whichever team has the most visible socks in its lineup. If any of its players is wearing high socks with stirrups, I will root for them to win by ten runs.

Of course, it has been a long time since the Chicago American Leaguers wore white socks. Remember the Richie Allen era, when the White Sox wore red socks, with a picture of two little white socks on them? Have you heard of the Everett AquaSox of the Northwest

League? They wear black socks, but: they have aqua in their caps. There used to be Blue Sox in Utica, but they got run out of town. What about the Colorado Springs Sky Sox? If you go to the team's website, you will find that they got new uniforms in 2008. The clothing is described in great detail, except for the socks. You would have thought that a team named for its socks would find it interesting to describe that item of clothing. Well, I guess we will just have to imaging what colour the sky is over Pike's Peak.

As for the Wenatchee Applesox – your guess is as good as mine. I grew up in apple country just north of there, and we had apples of many colours. With the Red Sox's Triple-A affiliate, it is easy. PawSox is just an alternate nickname. They are really the Red Sox with paws. Hmm.

(Yikes! I just found out about the Augusta Green Jackets.)

Now I know there are the Bowie Bay Sox. I have seen the water around Baltimore, so I don't even want to know what colour the capital's socks are.

(Yikes! And the Fort Wayne TinCaps!)

In fact, I'd like to stay in Maryland, and go back in time and sprawl in the bleachers at Bugle Field and watch the Baltimore Black Sox. In the years just before my birth they had a "million dollar infield," back when a million dollars was something, i.e. in the Great Depression. The nickname meant what those four Black Sox players would have been worth if they had been white guys.

SPIT

I learned how to hit the curve ball away. I learned how to charge the ball to make a double play. I learned how to put my cap on the way African Americans do. But I could never catch on to how you spit.

Baseball players have to spit a lot. Softball players almost as much. It's a good thing that basketball players don't have to spit. I guess that's because they sweat so much. It doesn't matter if ice hockey players spit, because it gets frozen quickly. Football players just have to remember to lift their face-guards out of the way. I guess tennis players can spit, depending on the surface they're playing on. Golfers don't seem to spit much, though they have kilometers of outdoors at their disposal. Boxers spit water into an old bucket between rounds. Soccer players? Who watches soccer?

But baseball players have to spit. I just couldn't get the hang of it. Usually I couldn't get a big-enough gob. If I did get a big-enough gob, it would wind up on the front of my shirt. I watched ballplayers spitting on television. Some of them could spit between their teeth, often in a kind of ratatat sequence. I watched Reggie Jackson. Boy, could he spit, I thought. Then I found out that he wasn't spitting spit – he was spitting Spitz. You know, sunflower seeds. As a kid I liked sunflower seeds, but I would hold one at a time up to my teeth and snap it open and take the little seed out from inside the shell, and throw the shell out the window or into a garbage can. But I watched Reggie, and what he did was, he'd pop a handful at a time into his mouth, hold them in one cheek, and work a seed at a time up to his front teeth, and snap it and spit the seeds out. Looked good on television.

Well, by the time I was in the Kosmic League I knew how to do that. I was Reggying at shortstop and on the bench and even while taking my slyly menacing stance in the right-handed hitter's box. I took the time to mentor my younger teammates on seed spitting. I tried not to salivate too much, not to get a soggy ball of seeds in my cheek.

I was watching the Little League World Series on TV the other night. Boy, some of those six-foot, 200 pound kids really knew how to spit spit before they went up to bat with their batting gloves and shin protectors and black stuff under their eyes. I saw one California kid spit three times on the way from the on-deck circle to the plate. He struck out. Then he spit again on the way back to the dugout. I would have run out of saliva before strike two.

STADIA

Some ballparks look better inside than they do from outside. Unfortunately, there are others that prove the opposite. Of course, a domed stadium means that if you look upward you might as well be in a hockey rink or some other such sad place.

I am particularly interested in what you can see if you look over the center field fence. Among urban major league parks, Pittsburgh's PNC Park is a winner, though the team that plays there sets records of futility even while they share a lot of the players on my fantasy team. From a lot of the seats you can see three of the bridges that cross the Allegheny River, and those bridges are painted yellow to match the Pirates' uniforms.

I like a lot of the ballparks in the west because you can see mountains or at least hills from them. A good example is Spring Mobile Ballpark in Salt Lake City. Other than Liberty Park, it is the only place in the city you'd like to be. It's one of the largest yards in Triple-A ball, but if you look outward you'll see something larger and just as pretty, that being a little mountain range called the Wasatch Front. The park is also conveniently located near the I-80, which will take you safely out of town and eastward toward the beautiful cities of Wyoming.

People always ask you what ballparks you like and what ballparks you hate. Remember when you used to just list, in the second category, those 60s-70s multisport circles that marred many eastern and middle-western cities? Jim Kaat had them in mind when he famously (but where?) said, "Every ball park used to be unique. Now it's like women's breasts – if you've seen one, you've seen both."

All right, here are three MLB stadia I didn't like. Candlestick Park, where they frisked you for weapons, and where thuggish-looking people attended in sleeping bags to protect them against the August chill. Yankee Stadium, which smelled like a sewer, and in which you felt an unnamed dread. And the big thing in Toronto, whose seats slope back so shallowly, that the fifteenth row is about a kilometer from the baseline. I even preferred that big pinball machine known as the Kingdome to the Toronto thing.

When it comes to minor league parks, and especially Single-A fields, I can forgive just about everything but backless concrete seats. I guess the worst stadium I have been in, if you can call it that, was essentially an American Legion park in Missoula, where the Osprey fly. The grandest was Dayton's Fifth Third Field, where they sell out in February. My favourite these days is tidy little Gesa Stadium, where the Tri-City Dust Devils play in Pasco, Washington. When the state gave the owners over a million dollars to spend, they built a huge sun shield to offer relief for the fans that were used to being baked while watching their North West League leaders.

You will notice that I haven't said anything about the sad decline in the names of ballparks.

But all right, I will tell you what my favourite MLB stadium is. It's Fenway, of course. The most fun I ever had at a big league game was in the bleachers at Wrigley. But I have been a Red Sox fan for all but the first ten years of my life, and though Seattle's Safeco is a lot more comfortable, there are few sights more interesting than watching a Boston left fielder use his bare hand to grab a ball that has rebounded from the Green Monster and nab or frighten a runner at second base.

TELEVISION

We have a television set for two reasons. We rent movies, including lately all the movies about Wyatt Earp. And we watch baseball games. The main rule is to try to get a game with the Dodgers or Red Sox in it. Almost as important a rule: choose a National League game if you can get one. Third: try to get a game featuring one or more of my fantasy league players, especially the pitchers.

So it is not that television is totally reprehensible. Cell phones and mp3 players are almost totally reprehensible. The DH is totally reprehensible. Lately I have gone to games between two minor league teams with National League associations, and these games included a couple of DHs. Still, I would rather watch a game between the Boise Hawks and the Yakima Bears at Yakima County Stadium than a game between the Giants and the Dodgers in my TV room.

But television has a lot to answer for. We all know that since the arrival of television, highschool kids no longer know what the preterite is. In fact now their teachers don't know what the preterite is. In fact, the person who made the program I am typing this page with doesn't know that there is such a thing as the preterite. Otherwise there would not be a wavy red line under it on this screen.

I left the beautiful Okanagan Valley before television arrived there. I remember that when you went across the line you would see tall TV antennae rising from shacks around Oroville and Tonasket, Washington, but those were just what were called in those days status-objects. In those days every town alongside the beautiful Okanagan River had a town baseball team and a grandstand to watch it from. A few years later those teams were gone, and the grandstands rotted, and Sundays were dead quiet alongside the river. All the people were inside, watching the Baltimore Orioles on television.

I think that almost all the riverside grandstands all across Canada and through the USA fell into rotted heaps after television arrived. And those erstwhile baseball fans were just as likely to be watching game shows as ball games. The other day I was looking at the list of teams in the St. Louis Cardinals farm system in 1946. In Triple-A they had the Rochester Red Wings. In Double-A they had the Houston Buffaloes. In Class A they had the Columbus Cardinals. In Class B they had the Decatur Commodores, the Allentown Cardinals, and the Lynchburg Cardinals. In Class C they had the Fresno Cardinals, the Winston-Salem Cardinals, the Duluth Dukes, the Pocatello Cardinals and the St. Joseph Cardinals. In Class D they had the Johnson City Cardinals, the Salisbury Cardinals, the Albany Cardinals, the Carthage Cardinals, the Marion Cardinals and the Hamilton Cardinals. I don't need to tell you that though they have one of the best farm systems in baseball, they don't have anywhere near as many young men in the field.

I blame television for that. Oh, and also for Jay Leno.

THOMSON

Being a fan of the Dodgers and the Red Sox all my life, I have at least two valid reasons for hating New York. When I was a kid the Yankees were always beating the Dodgers in the World Series, so I would wonder what's the use of playing 154 games just to have this happen again. Later, the Yankees would become the main obstacle in the path of my dear Sox. And the Giants? Well, you could not really hate them, but you could sure root against them, especially if they were your father's team and used to be really good, apparently.

When Bobby Thomson hit his so-called "Shot heard 'round the world" off Ralph Branca at the Polo Grounds on October 3, 1951, we heard it three time zones 'round the world, at Southern Okanagan High School, on the PA system in Mr. Fleming's math class. It was the third and deciding game. My heart felt like sewage in my chest. I think Mr. Fleming was a Giants fan. He grinned like one of Satan's fallen friends. When I got home I told my father that if he started chanting "The Giants win the pennant! The Giants win the pennant! etc" I would pack my scant belongings and leave home. My father grinned hopefully.

In history class just a few days before we had been told that the "Shot heard 'round the world was the one that a Bosnian Black Hand guy had started World War I with. But in a poem I had been reading outside class some Yank poet said that the original loud shot was heard at the start of what the US called their revolution. Well, here's what I wish. I wish it had been Branca's fastball bouncing off Bobby Thomson's head. I mean as long as it didn't involve Thomson getting hurt. I wish it had just been responsible for knocking the "p" out of him.

Bobby Thomson. Give me a break. He was a Scotchman, for Pete's sake! Okay, he moved to New York when he was two. But come on, a Scotchman! There's a ballpark in Edinburgh called Bobby Thomson Field. They can have it.

There are a lot of oh-no moments in one's baseball memory. If Willie McCovey had hit his line drive an inch or two higher, the Giants would have won the 1962 World Series, and more important, the Yankees wouldn't have. If Bill Buckner, whom I really liked up to that moment, had taken himself out of the game, he would not have muffed Mookie Wilson's grounder, and the Red Sox would have won the 1986 World Series. In 2009 Buckner was signing baseballs in the concourse of Nat Bailey Stadium in Vancouver. The signatures all look a little scrabbly because he kept dropping the ball.

But to get back to playoff games – the guy I would like to have locked in the clubhouse toilet was Bucky Dent. In Boston to this day he is known as Bucky "Fucking" Dent, because he hit a home run in the 1978 American League East Division tiebreaker playoff, to advance the Yankees and put sewage in Bosox hearts again. What made it so sad is that Bucky Dent was five feet one inch tall, weighed 110 pounds, and batted ninth in the Yankee lineup. His home run was really a typical popup that got caught in the wind and cleared the Green Monster by the width of a cockroach, which Dent is. At least Bobby Thomson hit 32 homers in 1951. Bucky "Fucking" Dent hit 40 in a twelve-year career.

Here's another way of looking at it. In August 1951 the Dodgers were 13.5 games ahead of the Giants. In July 1978 the Red Sox were 14.5 games ahead of the Yankees. There shouldn't have been any tiebreakers to start with. You might like New York in June, but I hate New York in late September.

TIGERS

I got my first big league team to be a fan of when I listened to the 1945 World Series on my Uncle Red's big console radio with the mysterious word "FM" on it, plus a lot of foreign cities like Peking and Moscow where you could not listen to Peking or Moscow. I was a Detroit Tigers fan for one year, switching then to the heart-breaking Boston Red Sox.

Through the forties and fifties everyone else was a fan of Bob Feller, so of course my favourite pitcher was Hal Newhouser. I kind of liked all those Tigers pitchers – Virgil Trucks, Dizzy Trout, Fred Hutchinson. But I was especially interested in Art Houtteman, because he was irregular. I have always had a soft spot for irregular ballplayers, like Leo Durocher, and Art Houtteman. When I retired from teaching university English and had to clear out my office, I pulled a picture of Art Houtteman off my bulletin board.

Before I ever saw a major league baseball game, I saw a professional game in Mexico City. This happened in the summer of 1964, when I went with my pal Sergio Mondragón to see the hometown Tigres play the visiting Pericos de Puebla. For the rest of the summer I was a *fanatico* for the Tigres de México. My Buddy Willy was with me in Mexico but he didn't go to baseball games.

If I had gone to Japan, as my buddy Willy did a few years before that, I would probably have wound up a follower of the Hanshin Tigers, a team that was born in the same year in which I was. Willy lived in Osaka, where the Tigers played. They changed their name from the Osaka Tigers to the Hanshin Tigers while he was there. He never saw them play.

Growing up, I always had favourite players of the then present, mainly Ted Williams, and of all-time. Most people I knew picked Babe Ruth as their all-time favourite, so I chose Ty Cobb. I liked his determined competitiveness and refusal to give up. When I found out that he didn't read because it might harm his eyes, I started to doubt. When I found out that he was a total gun-carrying racist asshole, I dropped him altogether. I liked my Tigers to be more like George Kell, even though he robbed Ted Williams of a batting crown.

In Montreal I played shortstop for the York Street Tigers. We were in a two-team league, and generally finished second.

The Detroit Tigers are tied with the New York Yankees for having the best home uniforms in baseball. It even looked classic on Mark Fidrych, one of the irregulars. It almost looked good on Denny McLain.

It looked good on Earl Wilson, who pitched against my Red Sox at Tiger Stadium in the first major league game I ever saw. That was in 1967. The Bosox won the pennant that year. The Tigers won it the following year. I saw them the next time I went to Detroit, enduring one of their 119 losses in 2003. At Comerica Park. Some things do change, too much.

TOMORROW

Yes, I remember that supporters of the Brooklyn Dodgers used to say, around the second week of October: "Wait till next year!"

But that is a special case. Baseball is usually the one sport in which fans can solace themselves with the fact that there's another chance to win tomorrow. After a football game, tomorrow means doing whatever you can to ease the sore parts of your body. After a basketball game tomorrow means waking up in another city and going to practice. After a hockey game, tomorrow means – well, who cares? It's hockey.

If you went 0 for 4 today and threw one wide of first, there is tomorrow. Tomorrow you will get two extra-base hits and start a highlight reel double play. Or if you are a team, tomorrow you will come back and give yourself a chance to take the series two games to one. If you are a fan, you have a good feeling about tomorrow. Your stopper is pitching tomorrow, and he goes particularly well against those guys. It's a day game tomorrow and your guys are over .500 in day games. Also, they're due.

Baseball fans are among the most optimistic people in the western world. Well, except for Mets fans. We were at the second-last game ever played at Shea Stadium, and the local fans were preparing themselves for the Mets' annual September swoon. There was a jolly cynicism in the upper deck behind home plate at Shea Stadium.

"Nice game, you guys," says the manager in the post-game dressing room, unless he is Lou Piniela, "we'll get them tomorrow.

Branch Rickey, possible the wisest man ever to get involved with building baseball teams, once said this about winning a World Series: "It's as inevitable as tomorrow but perhaps not as imminent."

When it comes to September, baseball fans and fantasy team owners pay a lot of attention to the magic number, the one for their team and the one for each of their rivals. Even when another team has reached the magic number zero, your true fan or fantasy team owner is interested in what could happen in tomorrow's game. In some circles this is called manic obsessive behavior disorder.

Even if you are a National League fan as I am, and if you have to have an American League, a Red Sox fan, you have to have a lot of respect for Dave Steib, even if he did pronounce his name as "Stieb." Only Jack Morris won more games than Steib did in the Eighties. He pitched for a Blue Jays team that was a few years short of their championship form. In two consecutive appearances in 1988 he lost no-hitters with two out in the ninth inning, and two strikes on the batter. In 1989 he had a perfect game broken up with two out in the ninth. Finally, in early September of 1990, he got what should have been at least his fourth no-hitter, a 3–0 job against the Cleveland Indians. He walked four.

Here is why I like Dave Steib. His 1986 autobiography was called *Tomorrow I'll be Perfect*.

TRIPLE

In the 1958 movie *The Vikings* Tony Curtis never did say, "Yonduh lies duh gastle of my foawdduh," but in the 1956 movie *Trapeze*, when Burt Lancaster, who plays a crippled former trapeze genius, asks Tony why he has come to him, Tony replies, "Beguzz you are duh only one dat can teach me duh dripple." It just goes to show: if you have no liking for a Viking, go to a cripple to learn the triple.

Okay. Sorry. I won't let it happen again.

As you know, the number three is very important in baseball. So, as you would expect, anything to do with a triple is going to be exciting. The triple crown of hitting, for example. Every few years, around June, say, sports writers who don't have enough to do, notice that some guy is leading the league in homers and runs batted in, and is third in the league in batting average. Pretty soon the columns appear, touting this guy's chance of being the first person since Carl Yastrzemski to capture the elusive triple crown. In 2009 it was Albert

Pujols, who has achieved just about every other honour it is possible to achieve with a Louisville Slugger or whatever club they are using these days. Yaz's feat was accomplished in the Red Sox's miracle year of 1967, and I always felt as if it were a tiny bit smudged by the fact that Harmon Killebrew tied him with 44 home runs.

Oh, by the way, Yaz got four triples that year.

People pay attention to the number of homers a fellow gets during a season. They often notice the number of doubles he piles up. They will pay attention to his hits total, 200 being a magic level. But I have never noticed baseball writers, broadcasters or fans paying all that much attention to the guy's triple total. But look: a triple is more exciting to watch than a single or a double. It's the kind of hit a batter usually doesn't have yet when he is going for the cycle. My fantasy team shortstop Jimmy Rollins disappoints the heck out of me most years, but in 2007 he had his MVP year, leading the National League in games, plate appearances, and at bats, getting his highest ever batting average at .296, amassing 212 hits, 38 doubles, 30 home runs, 94 RBI at the leadoff position, and 41 stolen bases in 47 attempts. But you know what impressed me the most? He had 20 triples.

Of course Ty Cobb holds the career record for triples at 295. No wonder he was the only person to hold records in hitting and running.

I will tell you one thing more exciting than a triple – Ichiro Suzuki making a throw from the right field foul pole and throwing the runner out at third. Without a hop. I saw this in Seattle one night. The third base umpire was so startled that he called the runner safe.

In 2009 I was lucky enough to see a triple play finished just a few feet in front of my face. I was sitting behind the home plate screen on closing day in Vancouver. With runners at first and third, a Vancouver Canadian hitter named Myrio Richard hit a hopper to third to start a typical double play, but then the runner at third, a slow-moving catcher named Max Stassi, elected rather late to head for home, where he was pronounced out on a throw from first. The Everett AquaSox lost the game, but turned in their first ever triple play.

I was involved in just such a play by the Granville Grange Zephyrs in the Kosmic League back in the Seventies. I started the play at short with a flip to Engledink Birdhumper at second, who fired to first baseman Glen Toppings, who in turn flung the pelota home where Cat Fisher, our diminutive catcher sealed the deal. What a proud moment!

UMPIRES

Some of the pregame stuff I could do without. I see no reason, for example, to have someone sing patriotic anthems before a sporting event. When I am waiting for a ball game in a US stadium I can hardly keep still while the locals are standing there with their right hands over their left nipples while a young white woman puts as many diphthongs as possible in "José can you see?" hoping, perhaps, to be mistaken for a young black songstress. I know that I am among the brainwashed, but it takes me aback every time. Sometimes it is worse – sometimes they have guys in military uniforms carrying flags and lethal weapons in from center field.

But I am a fan of a pregame item that hardly anyone shuts up to hear – the PA announcement of the umpires for tonight's game. When those names are announced I clap my hands and shout, "Yay!" Invariable, I am the only person in the crowd to do so. By now I have forgotten whether I do this sarcastically or genuinely. But it is in my nature to encourage those who don't get enough encouragement. I also often announce that Randolph Scott and Walter Matthau were the greatest Hollywood film actors of all time.

I often think about my father when I think about umpires. In his day, and by default in mine, a person who played baseball and softball often did some umpiring. It was part of the game, of what people nowadays would probably call the baseball culture. I saw my dad ump just about as often as I saw him catch or coach. I think that I got a good lesson in honesty and fairness from watching my dad ump.

So I like the umpires I remember from the olden days more than I like the umpires today. Of course just about everything today is going to Helena hand basket. When I was young (have you heard a baseball fan say those words?) the umpires wore jackets and ties, and they just looked as if they commanded respect while at the same time approaching invisibility. If someone like Leo Durocher threw his cap on the ground and kicked dirt onto the plate, the umpire would watch stoically if not impassively until the goof was finished, and then restart the game. Sometimes he would throw the goof out of the game, and if you were listening to the game on radio the announcer would say that Leo (or Casey) had said the magic word.

Nowadays the umpires in short sleeve shirts look as if they are looking for a confrontation or perhaps some attention. A guy who has just struck out looking just has to whisper "fiddle dee dee," before slouching to his dugout, and some hefty arbiter will whip off his mask, stick his chest out, run after the whiffee, and start shouting at him, before throwing him out of the game.

Well, we know that ballplayers on the road get a daily meal allowance about equal to the food budget of fifty Nigerian extended families, while umpires, who are always on the road, have to make do with Taco Bell. You would be pretty resentful of a twenty-five-year-old millionaire, too. But the game is for the people in the stands, after all. Most of these people are here to watch the ballplayers – except for that one guy cheering the names of the ump.

UNIFORM

Under a jumble of other great clothing in my closet I have Carmen Castillo's pants.

In case you don't remember Carmen Castillo, I'll remind you

that he was an outfielder from San Francisco de Macoris, Dominican Republic, a long way up the road from the shortstop factory at San Pedro de Macoris. In the 1980s Castillo would get about 200 at bats a year for the Cleveland Indians. I have the trousers from his road uniform in the early eighties. You remember those double-knits with no belt loops. These pants have a lot of sewing that indicate that Carmen used to slide into second on his right cheek.

I bought these trousers cheap at the Cleveland Indians shop in Cleveland in the mid eighties. From then until my unfortunate retirement in 2004 I wore them while starring as an infielder for the Paperbacks in the renowned Twilight League of Vancouver. These, despite the fabric, were proper baseball pants, not those baggy things that flop around the feet of too many ballplayers today. I wore them with sanitaries and stirrups, though the latter were never the colour of the grey Indians garb with the deep blue and red stretch belt and piping. I wore my high socks in blue and yellow, or solid orange. I was not a power hitter but I was a power dresser.

There were a lot of uniform parts in the Twilight League, but they were not what you might call "uniform." Our number one pitcher Jim liked to work in hospital scrubs and a 1915 glove and a huge afro in which it was rumoured that he kept devices for doctoring the ball. The number one pitcher of our rivals The Friendly People pitched in bare feet, which took nerve, because the park we played in was shared with junkies who tossed their needles rather than risk sharing them.

If any team in the Twilight League were to show up in uniforms with the name of a bank on them, for example, they would be laughed out of the park. We were not company slo-pitch dudes. We were know-it-alls with irony and fantasy lives.

Actually, a year or so before I made my much-regretted retirement from the Paperbacks, we did get uniform shirts. One of the new guys on the team happened to work in a place where they printed tee-shirts, so pretty soon our whole outfit had free tee-shirts. On the front was a ballplayer making a great running catch with an open book instead of a glove. On the back was a number. I got number 27, of course, nine times three, a kind of magic that befitted my talent with a glove.

Once in a while more than 70% of our players would remember to come to the game in these shirts.

UP

After I broke my hip and got four steel pins put into it when I was sixty-eight, I had to shut down my ball-playing career. It was just too difficult for me to accept that the blazing speed of foot that I was known for had been taken away from me.*

I like watching baseball on television. I like listening to it on the radio if I get the chance. I like driving all over the continent to see professional ball games at all levels. I like my fantasy league, even though I have been cruelly served by key injuries this year and deprived of the pennant my shrewd scouting should have got me.

But I miss playing ball like crazy. I miss the camaraderie, of course, and I miss the insults tossed back and forth between teams. But more than that I miss waking up on Sunday and seeing the sunshine out there and remembering that we're going to play the Write Sox today. I miss stretching to snaffle a high throw from third. I miss keeping track of the count and getting ready to go at the pitch. But most of all I miss being up.

To bat, I mean. If you can imagine, there were guys on my team that had to be reminded when it was their turn to get into the batter's box. I always had a bat in my hands when I was in the hole and we already had two out. When I was on deck I was always watching their pitcher carefully, checking his delivery, figuring out his pattern of pitches, location, speed.

When it comes to the normal morning, I am not good at getting up. I don't like it, but I do it. I hardly ever take recreation drugs anymore, so I don't get up like that, not even on uppers. I am often in airplanes, but I get no thrill being up. I am a pretty old gink now, but I don't have a great deal of trouble getting up, especially if I get some help. But when you have to retire from the diamond, you know you're up against it. You're in extra innings with no expectation of winning.

Life, as they told us early in the game, has its ups and downs. But I have to say that there really isn't a nicer up than being up to bat in a ball game. Assuming the stance you've been working on. Taking a practice swing. Making a wisecrack if the situation seems to call for one. Telling yourself to watch the ball from the time that the chucker gets it into his hand. Reminding yourself to hit behind the runner. Now I will tell you what I went up there looking for: a pitch at just about any altitude but on or just off the outside corner. I loved hitting that ball down the right field foul line. In my fifties I could still get to second on that hit. In my sixties I enjoyed the challenge of getting to first before the right fielder's throw did. Heh.

If they asked me whether I would rather see Venice again or get to bat against Marke Andrews again, I'd choose being up.

*He'd usually get to first base on a triple – Jean Baird.

UTICA

I don't remember how I came into it, but I once owned a complete set of baseball cards for the Utica Blue Sox for the year 1996. The Blue Sox were a short season Single-A team in the New York-Pennsylvania League. Over the years I have sent the cards one by one stuffed into letters to people who may have just chucked them out. I don't have any left, so I don't know whether any of those young hopefuls made it to the Show. After the 2001 season the Ripkins bought the team and moved them to Maryland, where they became the Aberdeen Ironbirds. The New York-Pennsylvania League also has teams in Vermont, Massachusetts, and Ohio.

I have never been a real collector of baseball cards. I did not play throw against the wall with them when I was a kid, and I did not attach one to my bike spokes to make motorcycle noises. I was not much excited about the big trading card rage manufactured in the early nineties. When nudniks started putting their Mickey Mantles in their safety deposit boxes, I shrugged. When they started putting fibres from Mickey mantle's jersey in the cards I would have spit if I'd known how. When they started making trading card sets of the first Gulf War, I prayed that the bubble would burst. I was pretty happy when the trading card shop windows were covered with yellowing newspapers.

Speaking of bubbles. When I was a kid you got a whole pile of bubble gum and a few baseball cards. One day I noticed that you got one little stick of bubble gum and quite a few cards. I don't remember when it was that the gum disappeared altogether, and kids were being bamboozled into buying fancily-packaged sets of player cards. I didn't buy any of those, but as a purported adult during the late eighties, I would buy a pack of gum from time to time, mainly for chawing at my softball games. Just about every pack I bought contained a picture of John Kruk in a San Diego Padres uniform.

I did have the odd moment, though. One time I was doing a reading at Bentley College in Waltham, Massachusetts, and was enjoying a nice big meal and drinks at an attractive bar-restaurant with a bunch of interesting people after the reading. Such occasions are the real reason for going on reading tours, and perhaps a good reason to keep on writing books. During the course of the celebration it became known that the good-looking woman across the table from me was a Ted Williams fan. Well, so am I.

I was working on my impulsiveness in those days, so I downed the first half of my latest drink, and then quietly departed the bar. I figured that there would be a trading card shop a block or two away, and sure enough, there was. I found a Ted Williams card sealed in plastic for, I don't remember, maybe $16, and bought it. I carried it back to the bar carefully, as if it were a rose, and presented it to the good-looking woman. Then I drank the rest of my current drink, the perfect impulsive Canadian poet.

UZBEKISTAN

At Uppsala you would think that they would be smart enough to play baseball, because it's the oldest research university in Scandinavia, and for centuries it has been one of the most renowned places of learning in Europe. But when it comes to non-scholarly pursuits, the students do not go in for sports at all, preferring music.

In Uganda they used to have a President for Life who had previously been the country's heavyweight boxing champion. He was also a terrifying figure with a rugby ball in his hands. It's too bad they aren't wise enough to have baseball in Uganda. He would have been an amazing DH.

In Ulan Bator they are tremendously proud of their national stadium, but a careful scanning of a city map will not turn up a baseball park. It appears that the Mongolians spend most of their energy and sports tugrugs on wrestling and yak races.

In Uttar Pradesh they are sort of coming close. Though India's official national sport is field hockey, the folks in the country's fifth-biggest state prefer cricket. Over the winter of 2008–2009 the Pittsburgh Pirates signed two young Indian pitchers who came first and second in a national throwing contest. They had developed powerful shoulder muscles by throwing javelins – in Uttar Pradesh.

A third of major league baseball players are from Latin America, but so far none of them is from Uruguay. If you go on the Internet and look for youth baseball camps in Uruguay you will come up with no results. But when we were in Argentina a couple years ago, we found that their Little League season had just ended.

In the province of Udine, a nice place you can go through on your way to Trieste, the city that has haunted my life, there is a town in the Italian Winter League called Cervignano. The Cervignano Tigers are not the powerhouse of the league, but they have a nice little park with a short right field.

They have been working on baseball for twenty years in Ukraine.

They have Little League, which is in need of equipment and landscaping. And they have had senior teams that compete in the European Baseball Championship. In 1995 and 2007 they finished in 9th place, their highest finish so far. They are better than Malta.

The republic of Upper Volta is now called Burkina Faso. It has a lot of languages besides French, and it is surrounded by a lot of other countries, and it has no seashore. Being a former French colony, it plays a lot of soccer. Tennis is also pretty popular. Burkina Faso used to compete in the Davis Cup, but after losing all their games, the national team decided not to do that any more. They did not, though, turn to baseball.

And what about Uzbekistan? Their national pastime is kok-boru. It's a team sport performed on horseback. The object is to get your horse into full gallop and then lean down and grab the headless carcass of a goat, get a clear run to the goal line, and once there to pitch it over the line into a vat. The game would probably go over well in Kansas City, where, as in Uzbekistan, not much baseball is played.

VALENZUELA

Do you remember Ritchie Valens? He was a left-handed kid from the San Fernando Valley, who taught himself to play a guitar right-handed, and became a music star and the first hero of Mexican-American rock-and-roll. His recording career took off early in 1959, with the smash hits "Donna" and "La Bamba," and it ended the night the music died in Iowa on February 3 that year. Buddy Holly and the Big Bopper died with him. The Big Bopper was 28 years old. Buddy Holly was 22. Ritchie Valens was 17. His full name was Richard Steven Valenzuela. His manager changed the last name to Valens in order to broaden his appeal to "white" Americans. In the US, apparently, Mexicans are "coloured" or something.

The next Valenzuela to make it big in Los Angeles and the USA was also left-handed. His name was Fernando, just like the valley that Ritchie was born in, but he was born in the state of Sonora, almost two years after that plane crash in Iowa. When he joined the Los Angeles Dodgers for the 1981 season he embarked on the most illustrious rookie pitching feat since Mark Fidrych's amazing debut of 1976. If the middle third of the 1981 season had not been lost to a players' strike, there is no telling what Fernando would have done. As it was, he went 13–7, with a 2.48 ERA and a league-leading 180 strikeouts. He won the rookie of the year award and the MVP, and led the Dodgers to a World Series crown.

The Mexican-American crowd filled Dodger Stadium when Fernando made one of his starts. A phenomenon that the media dubbed "Fernandomania" swept the country, filling ballparks all over the National League, and making trading card dealers rich. People such as I loved turning on the television and watching this (let's face it) fat guy looking up to the heavens and whiffing a Cub. It was fun that he couldn't say much in English, not even "doughnut," and it was really fun that he thought he was Babe Ruth at the plate. During his rookie season he hit his only lifetime triple, but in 1990 he batted .204 and had a .730 OPS!

I never got to see Fernando play in real life, but Jean and I did manage to see Fernando Valenzuela Jr. play a couple of times. Fernando Junior is built the way his father was, he has his father's face, and he too is left-handed, but he is a first baseman. In 2003, after playing great ball for UNLV, he spent the summer with the Eugene Emeralds, San Diego's team in the short-season A Northwest League. We saw him play a game in Vancouver, and then eleven days later in Boise. I don't remember how he fared.

Here is something odd. It is not that Valenzuela is an unusual name. There is a city next to Manila named Valenzuela. One of South America's major writers is the Argentine novelist Luisa Valenzuela. There is a rock singer named Jesse Valenzuela, but he's no Ritchie. There are jockeys and professors and economists. But except for a third baseman who had 14 at bats for the Cardinals in 1958, Fernando was the family's only major leaguer.

The last I heard, Fernando Jr. was playing in the Mexican League.

VETERANS

By 2000 I had been a veteran for thirty-five years. One of the funniest things that happened to me around then was getting hit in the eye and blinded by a line drive in front of the bag at third. A young guy on the team we were playing, the Secret Nine, was talking on his cell phone to an ambulance attendant. The latter must have asked him how old the victim was. The young guy said I was in my thirties. Gill Collins snorted and laughed, and informed the cub that I was well into my sixties.

But long before I joined the category I liked veterans of the game. In my present fantasy league I always have more players who are over forty than anyone else in the league. I learn my lesson by late July every year, but then come draft time in the new year I snap up Denny Moyer. Brian Fawcett, who owns a team in my league, often maintains that I have two or three dead guys on my roster. This is an exaggeration: I have never had more than one at a time.

Ted Williams was in the US military, and he voted Republican, I guess, but I just about loved him when he was a forty-year old outfielder for the Red Sox. In his fifth decade he was a better hitter than any 26-year-old in the American League. At the end of the 1960 season, Roger Maris, the Most Valuable Player, had an OPS of .952. He was twenty-six. Ted Williams was forty-two. His OPS was 1.096

There are two kinds of veterans I like. There's the old-timer who knows how to save and manage his energy, how to get rest and eat the right stuff and conserve his power for the moment when he'll need it. I like him. Then there's the greybeard who thinks that he can still pour it on, running at top speed into a fence, taking the turn at second base with none out, winding up in the whirlpool bath or on the trainer's table for hours before and after the game. I like him, too.

I love it when Tim Wakefield strikes out Robinson Cano with a knuckleball that disappears somewhere over Brockton. I love it when Randy Johnson gets a fastball past Prince Fielder. I loved it when 48-year-old Julio Franco stole second base. I go to a lot of independent league games, and keep hoping that I will see Satch warming up in the bullpen.

But maybe my favourite old codger was Luke Appling. His nickname was Old Aches and Pains, because all through his career he complained about his injuries and agonies, claiming that he didn't know whether he would be able to start today. White Sox teammates knew better than to ask him how he felt, because it would take him half an hour to tell them.

But in 1982, when he was 77 years old, he clubbed a home run off Warren Spahn's heat in an old-timers' game in RFK Stadium. It is true that the fence was in a ways, and the ball travelled only 250 feet or so. But here is a question for you: do you think you could have even hit Spahn's pitch?

VICTORIA

Baseball comes and goes in Victoria. It can't seem to stick, not even to stick as well as it does in Vancouver. Maybe this is because Victoria should be more suited to cricket. In fact, you can find people playing cricket in some park from time to time. Cricket, because Victoria sounds like cricket, maybe, that being a poetry concern. But more so because Victoria is always trying to persuade US American tourists that they are visiting a little bit of Olde England. So they present shoppes and beefeaters and hanging flowers and high tea at the Empress Hotel. It used to be a little more authentic before the cream came in little packages.

But before the Civil War was over in the USA, gold-rushers were playing baseball in Victoria. In 1866 a team called the Olympic Club taught the young men in the Victoria Cricket Club how to play the game, and the cricketers promptly clobbered them. A few years later there were teams all over town, some with baseball uniforms, some with outfield fences. Pretty soon players were being paid for their efforts. As early as 1901 the Victoria Baseball Club won the British Columbia Baseball Championship, a prize usually contended for by teams in New Westminster and Kamloops.

By 1905 baseball was all over town, and cricket would not get serious again until the Caribbean immigrants arrived decades later.

In 1905 Victoria got its first professional team, the Legislators of the Class B Northwestern League, but the games were played far beyond the reach of the streetcars, and the team moved to Spokane after three months. Amateur ball held sway until 1911, when the Victoria Islanders arrived, changed their name to the Bees, and continued till the Great War took all the young ballplayers to Europe. After the war there was a team called the Capitals, but after 1921 the city had to make do with amateurs for a couple of decades.

After the Second World War Victoria secured a franchise in the Class B Western International League, first as the Athletics, because they were playing at Royal Athletic park, and then as the Tyees. In 1949 Gil McDougald batted .344 for the Athletics, two years before winning the rookie of the year award over Minnie Minoso because McDougald played for the Yankees. I missed the Athletics, but in 1953 I came to Victoria, and saw some team playing in the park they had recently abandoned. It had a strange outfield fence that went almost straight across from foul line to foul line, so that the shortest homers were to center field.

Two decades later the professionals were back, as the Mussels and then the Blues contended from 1978 to 1980 in the Class A Northwest League, finishing behind teams like the central Oregon Phillies and the Gray's harbor Loggers. Then the amateurs, as well as the rugby players and cricketers, took over again until the ill-starred Canadian Baseball League played a half-season in 2003. The Victoria Athletics were the best draw in the eight-team independent league, but they finished last in the western division.

In 2009 pro ball was back, and I am proud to say that I travelled to Victoria along with my wife Jean Baird and the great poet George Stanley to witness the Golden League's new franchise the Seals take on the Long Beach Armada at the Athletic Park home opener. Okay, they blew an early lead and lost, and they did finish the season at the bottom of the Northern Division, but there is professional baseball in Victoria, which is more than you can say for Kansas City.

VINEGAR

I have found myself musing about Vinegar Bend Mizell lately. I don't know why. I think I got by for a few decades without thinking about him. Yes, he was a starry pitcher of sorts when I was a teen or less, but he wound up at 90–88 (though he had a pretty good ERA at 3.85).

I guess I have been thinking about him because of his nickname. When he arrived on the St. Louis Cardinals roster in the early fifties the newspaper guys (and I suspect Bob Broeg here) had a good time with him. He was an obvious country lad, born in Vinegar Bend, Alabama and raised in nearby Leakesville, Mississippi, with the given name of Wilber, a six-foot-four lefthander aged twenty-one who liked to wear his cap on the back of his head. Come on.

So I was wondering: what did Eddie Stanky and Solly Hemus call him? Vinegar? Vinnie? VB? What do you suppose an earlier bunch of Cardinals called Johnny Leonard Roosevelt Martin? Do you think they called him The Wild Horse of the Osage? Or maybe just Horse? Nope, they called him Pepper. Ball players use a lot of slang and other language that the sportswriters never report or even find out about. When it comes to clubhouse nicknames, chances are you will never find out what they are. Yes, Mr. Dean was addressed as Diz, but his brother was not called Daff. No Red Sox infielder ever said, "Hey, Splendid!" to his left fielder.

But I kind of miss the heyday of fanciful cognomens. Rapid Robert gave way to Bullet Bob. The Iron Horse was replaced by Ol' Double XX. As late as the 1970s No Neck Williams and Larvell Sugar Bear Blanks were patrolling major league outfields. Nowadays you don't get very many fanciful nicknames. Thank goodness for The Big Unit and The Big Hurt. But mainly we have to make do with catchers called Pudge and the other Rodriguezes called A-Rod and K-Rod and so on down the alphabet. Pretty dull.

Wilmer Mizell did not go back to Vinegar Bend to raise livestock or anything like that. He was a Republican congressman from one of the Carolinas until his party got torpedoed by the Watergate scandal. He's buried in whichever Carolina he was representing, and I don't know whether he ever went back and visited Vinegar Bend or Leakesville. The median income for a household in Leakesville is $26,000. In Vinegar Bend it's $30,000.

VOLCANOES

I was thinking of narrating a story that takes place in Visalia, where home plate is nearly at the backstop, but then they changed the team name from the Oaks to something more fierce, so I decided to go with the Volcanoes.

The Volcanoes stretch in a line from northern California to British Columbia. You've seen pictures of them, Mounts Shasta, Hood, Rainier, Baker, and Mount Saint Helens, etc. A while back the last-named one blew her top, possibly because the US American mapmakers would not provide her with an apostrophe.

The Volcano closest to Salem, the capital of Oregon, is Mount Jefferson, which last blew in 450 AD, when the Picts were marauding all the British towns left by the departed Romans. Much closer to Salem is a little burg named Keizer, where the Salem-Keizer Volcanoes play their home games in the short-season Northwest League. There are 150,000 people in Salem and 35,000 in Keizer, but for decades Keizer has been resisting incorporation into the bigger city. Until 1989 Salem had a team that played in the capital, but then they moved out of town until 1997, when the Bellingham franchise came south, and started to raise SF Giants babies.

In 2009 the Northwest League finals featured the two hyphenated squads, the Volcanoes prevailing over the Tri-City Dust Devils in four games. It was Salem-Keizer's third championship in four years. In fact, since coming back into the league, Salem (-Keizer) has won the western division of the league just about every year. Still, I always forget their name, often referring to the Kaiser-Wilhelm Volcanoes.

Or the Winston-Salem Witches. I mean, really – if the New York Giants can play in the state of New Jersey, surely the Salem Volcanoes could play in Keizer. The Saskatchewan Silver Sox currently play their home games in Yuma, Arizona, after all.

You have to take a narrow country road to get to the rinky-dink Volcanoes Stadium. There's chain-link fencing, backless seating, a pervading sense of cheapness all about, which seems strange for the site of so many playoff games. The I-5 runs right by the right field fence, and the train tracks are just the other side of that. You can hear traffic all game long. The scoreboard isn't much to write home or even third about, but there is a tiny plywood volcano on the fence in left-center, and if one of the locals gets a home run, a puff of smoke comes out of it.

There is one unusual feature greeting folks who schlep around ballparks as we do. The weekday night games start at 6:35. We thought it might be because of the narrow country road upon which people have to drive home a great distance. So we asked our neighbours, who were pointedly avoiding the lava dogs, a delicacy offered in the narrow concourse. Well, it turns out that people around there vote for things. They voted to call the team the Volcanoes, and they voted to start games at 6:35. Why is that, we enquired. You'll see when they get into our bullpen, a nice old lady told us. Sure enough. The first seven innings took about two hours. Then we got so see about eight pitchers from the home team's bullpen, and by the time we got onto the nearby I-5 games were over all up and down the Pacific Region.

WHOPPERS

In the Kosmic League I was such a swift base runner that I once hit a slow line drive that hit me on my way from first to second. I got the single, but was also the first out of the inning.

In the Twilight League I was playing first base. I read in a magazine that on a ground ball the first base umpire watched the bag for the runner's foot, and listened for the sound of the ball landing in the mitt. I practised and practised and at last was able to use my mouth to imitate the sound of a baseball plocking into a trapper. Then I had to learn to make perfectly silent catches. I got a heck of a lot of outs that way, and you should have seen the way those first base coaches would go into hysterics.

The aluminum bat had not yet been invented when I was catcher for the British Columbia team for our tournament at the Royal Canadian Air Cadets tournament at RCAF Abbotsford in the mid-fifties. In a game against Alberta I threw out two runners at second, but my most memorable defensive moment came in the semi-final game against Northern Ontario. The bad guys had the go-ahead run on at first with one out when the next hitter chopped one off the plate, breaking his bat while doing so. The ball went high in the air in fair territory, and the business end of the bat landed hard in my mitt. I could see that there would be no chance of beating the runner at first, but I could also see that the runner ahead of him had barrelled around second and was nearly to third base. I knew that I didn't have time to catch the ball when it came down and make the throw, so I swung at it with the near-bat I had in my hand, slapping a hard one-hopper to my third baseman, who just held the ball and let the runner slide into it. We won that game, but I broke my nose playing catch in the dark that night, and had to play left field next day. Saskatchewan beat us by two runs, and my nose was crooked as all get out.

You've seen golf on television? One of the standard shots is the long chip onto the green, where the ball lands beyond the pin, then stops and rolls back toward the hole. All the way through the Kosmic League days and the days in between and then most of the Twilight League days, I worked on that shot, only with an aluminum bat and a softball. First I figured out how to bunt it toward the third baseman and watch him charging a roller that is headed back toward the plate. Then I just about perfected the popup double. Let me describe this phenomenon. I wait for the pitch I need, a high fastball with not much on it. Then I pop it over the infield, usually into center field, where the center fielder thinks he has a one-hopper, only to change gears and run after a ball that is rolling toward second base, a location I have by this time taken up because I had double in my mind from the clink of the bat.

WILD

My friend Paul Naylor likes to discourage the visiting pitcher by shouting "Terrible pitch!" or especially "Crazy wild!" when said pitcher delivers a ball in the sky or the dirt. If you time your taunts well, you can make the pitchers and hitters hear what you are hollering in the stands at Nat Bailey Stadium in Vancouver.

Jean, my sweetheart and baseball companion, especially likes games that feature multiple errors, bonehead plays and extremely wild pitches. We go to a lot of Single-A games around the continent.

So naturally when I told her that I was getting to the W's in this book, she said that I had to do Wild.

Crazy wild, she said. The wild card, she said, the wild side of life. I was watching a game from the Metrodome yesterday, and she came into the room and said, "The Wild." I told her no, that is hockey, and like the Toronto Maple Leafs, we do not do hockey.

My favourite baseball movie is *Major League*, a brilliantly funny remake of *The Producers*. Instead of "Springtime for Hitler," they sing "Wild Thing," which is the nickname of the Cleveland Indians' ace hurler. It's true, the wild man on the mound has always electrified the sports page scribes and the fans. Think of Rex Barney. He won a total of 35 games over his career with the Dodgers, 15 of them in 1948. He pitched a no-hitter, sure, but he was mainly known for his fastball against the backstop. Think about Ryne Duren the Yankee reliefer with the pop bottle eyeglasses. His fastball was so fast that he buckled the knees of the guy in the on-deck circle. His eyesight was pretty bad. He once hit the guy in the on-deck circle. We remember Rex Barney and Ryne Duren because of their combination of speed and wildness.

Think of Randy Johnson, who stands eight feet tall and throws the ball at 120 MPH. He can slap your helmet with his follow-through. When he was with Seattle he led the league in walks three years in a row. In the third of those years he led the league in strikeouts, and did that eight more times. Now he hardly walks anyone. He bewilders them with fastballs on the corner. There are a lot of people who think that the Big Unit was more fun to watch in the olden days when no one in the Kingdome was safe from a beanball.

The word "wild" is related to the German word "wald," which means forest, just as the word "savage" comes from the Latin "silva," which also means forest. You know the forest – that's what the Mariners are waiting for someone to lead them out of.

Maybe the pennant race is a wild goose chase for some people.

WILLIAMS

You know that I think unhappily about 1951 when it comes to the terrible thing that happened in the National League and was then apparently heard around the world.

But I was fifteen that year, a prime time for kids growing up far from the big city, reading books and magazines and newspapers, and listening to the Seattle Rainiers or Sacramento Solons on the radio. I intended to be a snob, to listen to jazz and not what was then called western music, but how could you avoid Hank Williams? I did not want to admit that he was worth listening to, but I learned all the words to "Hey, Good Lookin'," a big hit in 1951, a year and a half before he died in the back seat of a Cadillac.

In 1951 there was no television in the Valley. There were two drive-in theatres up in Penticton, but who had a car? So we were stuck with whatever movie from the past year was currently playing at the Oliver Theatre on the main. Alex Gough, the Lou Costello look-alike who ran the Oliver Theatre was fond of Sonja Henie and Esther Williams (who was on the covers of all the magazines that year), so there we were in a town with no skating rink but a new swimming pool, watching such gems as *Take Me Out to the Ball Game*, which had been released in the big cities in 1949. It also starred Frank Sinatra and Gene Kelly, who didn't look much like baseball players to me. But secretly I loved it.

In those days I still followed boxing, and I can still hear that bell and Don Dunphy's voice. There was only one world champion in each weight division in those days, and there weren't as many divisions. So when the lightweight champ Ike Williams was upset by a pug like Jimmy Carter, even a kid in the sticks smelled a rat. Name was Blinky Palermo.

1951 saw the publication of a momentous book that I would not read until seven or eight years later. This was *The Autobiography of William Carlos Williams*, the poet/novelist/essayist I would take as my second father, though I would never meet him nor correspond with him, though I did get a letter from his widow in the sixties sometime. In one of his novels he wrote a wonderful chapter about a father and son going to a game at the Polo Grounds.

But you know whom I am leading up to, don't you? You know, I would later find out that he was probably a Republican, and that he probably killed a number of people in North Vietnam, but he also scolded the Baseball Hall of Fame for having no Black players memorialized in it. In 1951 he was in his 33rd year, coming back from a season in which he had played in only 89 games because he broke his elbow in the All-Star Game. He got 97 RBI in those 89 games. In 1952 he would be off to his second wartime pilot job, but in that in-between year he settled for what would be career years for most ball players: a .318 average, 30 homers, 126 RBI, and a telling statistic, 144 walks.

In 1951 there was a lot of competition, but the Red Sox' number 9 was my favourite Williams that year.

WORLD

US Americans have a strange idea of the world, or let us say that their idea of the world is a lot different from the world's. They have strange notions of smaller bits of geography, too. They call their country "America," for example. Well, back in the nineteenth century their patriots predicted a United States from "pole to pole." When you drive around in the USA you come upon signs such as "Garlic Capital of the World," or "World-Famous Hotdogs." It's no wonder then, that when Hollywood makes hundreds of movies about extraterrestrial creatures invading Earth, these creatures always arrive in the USA, usually within reach of Los Angeles. When Bug Eyed Monsters kidnap human beings for research, they always scoop up people in the USA, generally in the woods of New England.

When I was a kid the Pope of the Roman Catholic Church was always an Italian, and the World Champion boxers were always Americans. Once in a while another country could send a heavyweight to be a loser to Joe Louis or Muhammad Ali. But Luis Firpo or Brian London were never going to be World Champion. I mean if in 55 years only 7 of *Sports Illustrated*'s Sportsmen of the Year were not denizens of the USA, what can you expect? The rest of the world just cannot produce athletes who rank. Pelé? A bum. Bjorn Borg? Not a chance. Dick Tiger? Who he?

So you should not be surprised when you turn on the TV to watch the playoffs, and the Philadelphia Phillies are referred to over and over again as the "World Champions." The last time I looked the Japanese national team was the world champion team, having defended their title against Korea in Dodger Stadium in March of 2009. I don't recall that the Phillies played anyone after defeating Tampa Bay for the US championship.

Have a look at the situation in 2006. Sweden won the hockey championship in the winter Olympics and then won the world championship in Riga a few months later. Spain defeated Greece to win the world basketball championship in Tokyo. Japan defeated Cuba to take the world baseball championship in San Diego.

Yet in the spring of 2007 TV announcers in the US casually referred to St. Louis Cardinals as the world champions of baseball. But the last team the Cardinals played in the fall of 2006 was Detroit's. In 2007 too, those announcers referred to the "World Champion San Antonio Spurs," even though the Spurs had not played anyone after sweeping the Cleveland Cavaliers. In the spring I even heard those announcers laud the "World Champion Indianapolis Colts," as if the Super Bowl winners had had to knock down the challenge of, oh I don't know, the Beirut Bombers.

Now take Soccer. I agree, it's a boring game, but at least when soccer has a world cup, they let teams from six continents vie for it. The trophy doesn't look much like a cup. But I am wondering whether the Ohio newspapers are calling the Columbus Crew, holder of the Major League Soccer crown, the defending world's champs?

WYOMING

I drove across the top right corner of Wyoming on a motor trip westward in 1969, I think it was, and did not go there again until 2009 (unless you count the time my Denver-bound airplane had to set down in Cheyenne for a couple of hours while waiting for a blizzard to depart the Denver airstrip), when Jean and I drove to the other three corners on our annual baseball trip. In fact on that trip, which went from Vancouver to Denver and back, we slept in Wyoming in four different places, and how many people can say that? Strange. I mean Wyoming is famously thin when it comes to population, so how is it that a person has always known the names of so many cities there? Sheridan, Cheyenne, Laramie, Casper.

In 2003 we saw a ball game in Helena, where the visiting team was the Casper Rockies. This team had been, until two years earlier, the Butte Copper Kings, the poet George Stanley's favourite Pioneer League team. In 2008, though, due to the conventional fan vote, the team was rebranded the Casper Ghosts. As the only professional baseball team in the state, the Ghosts combine two functions: they are the advanced rookie league clinic for the Colorado Rockies, and they are, next to the National College Rodeo, the best family-oriented entertainment in town.

Casper is a nice town, too. Jean and I picnicked in one of the gorgeous green parks, and you really notice the work that went into the greenness when you see the brown plains and hills surrounding the city. We enjoyed our stroll alongside the North Platte River. I guess I was enjoying two towns, because I read a lot of western novels when I was a teenager. I kept my ear cocked to hear the real ghosts of Casper, the American Indians who were slaughtered by the US Army and others in the nineteenth century.

In case you are wondering about the spelling, I can tell you that the fort that preceded the city was named after a military gent whose middle name was Caspar, just like that of the ghost or the Magus (at least as he is represented in our language) who visited the baby Jesus. In the western US the spelling of place names tends to favour namers who were not big on history or language or pronunciation (see "Boise").

The Ghosts play their home games at Mike Lansing Field, thus called because outfielder Lansing was born in a little town nearby, and played his last big league season in 2001, just in time to be immortalized. The park has only 2500 seats but a huge playing area, with corners at 355 feet, to make up for the fact that Casper is a mile high.

I liked it. We saw a game between the last-place Ghosts and the second-to-last-place Ogden Raptors. The Ghosts are all hitting and no pitching. No Ghost pitcher won more than four games in 2009. I was lucky enough to gather my first Pioneer League ball, to add to my collection, and I had to pick up a team cap. The logo on the front of the cap is not a friendly ghost. He is a really mean looking spectre with a red gash across his silvery-white head, the gash having been stitched like a baseball. Oh, and it is the only professional team hat that glows in the dark. Jean wouldn't let me wear it to bed in our room at Yellowstone Park.

Oh, and what do you think the Casper mascot is? Wrong. He is a tall duckbilled platypus named Hobart. Next question.

X-GIANTS

In 1992 I was lucky enough to be in Arizona for spring training, and though I was surprised to find so many major-league games sold out, I snaffled seats to watch the Oakland A's minor-leaguers play against the Colorado Rockies minor leaguers. This was more than a year before the Colorado Rockies would play their first game ever. Then later in the year I was visiting the Hall of Fame at the end of a reading tour of the northeastern US, and while I was there I saw that the gift shop was selling Rockies jackets and Florida Marlins jackets. Well, I figured, purple isn't great, but it is better than that whatever it was, a kind of greenish bluish colour. I have been wearing that jacket for seventeen years now, and often. I recently wore it while watching a home game of the Rockies Rookie-A farm team Casper Ghosts.

I bought a hat at Cooperstown, too, because I am a baseball cap kind of guy. It was mainly white, with a black peak and a big orange X edged with black on the front. What is this, I asked. 1936 Cuban X-Giants, I was told. In African-American baseball about half the teams were called the Giants. For examples, there were the Chicago American Giants, the Washington Elite Giants, the Kansas City Giants, the Zulu Cannibal Giants, the Shreveport Acme Giants, the Baltimore Elite Giants, the Brooklyn Royal Giants, the Nashville Elite Giants, and many others.

The Cuban Giants were probably the first African-American professional baseball team. They came together first as the Black Panthers in Babylon, NY in 1885, and lasted for twenty years. There were no Cubans on the team, of course. In those days black players were called "Cubans" because there was no colour line in Cuban baseball, and this way white audiences could watch black guys playing ball and not feel a little funny. The ballplayers used to talk gibberish while they played, hoping to sound foreign.

Like a lot of things in Negro League baseball history, and even more things on Wickipedia, the story of the Cuban Giants and the Cuban X-Giants and the Authentic Cuban Giants is told in a lot of different ways, all having to do with ownership issues. In around 1891 the Cuban Giants players skedaddled and played as the Big Gorhams, but in 1896 E.B. Lamar Jr. bought the team and called them the Cuban X-Giants. Until 1907 they proved to be the best team in Black American baseball.

When the Negro Major Leagues got going in 1920, the Cuban X-Giants were not one of their teams called the Giants. Instead, there was a barnstorming team that was using the name and showing up all over the eastern half of the continent. Nowadays the retro sports outfitting stores offer variations of Cuban X-Giants regalia, and I have mine to go along with my Homestead Grays cap and my vintage Cienfuegos Elefantes jacket.

X-MEN

I don't know about you, but I am on the Facebook group Singapore Baseball. I have to tell you: it's not easy keeping up with the latest standings in the National Baseball League in that little Asian country. I have heard some players on Facebook mention recent games and scores, but the latest official stats I have show that my team, the X-Men, were in second place in the Woodlands Division as of September 7, 2008. But they had played just three games. The X-Men's best hitter, Devin Kay, had an OPS of 2.458.

I like just about everything I have found out about this team. The only disappointment I have so far is that their logo looks just like the New York Yankees one, with an X substituted for the Y and an M for the N. But look – here at their website is the first reference I find to the team: "by the power vested in us by Brewerkz Beer, the X-Men were created July 11th, 2003."

The X-Men play against the SAS Eagles, for example, at Kallang Ballpark, which is next to the National Stadium, or rather where the National Stadium, opened in 1973, was officially closed in 2007, to make way for a great new roofed stadium called the Sports Hub. Well, there have been delays, and two years after the great closing ceremony, they are still playing soccer at the National. 35,000 people came to the Nat to hear Michael Jackson in 1996. A lot of pop stars have performed there, and it has also been the site of several fires. The annual National Day Parade also takes place there, perhaps because the track oval is the longest clear road on the island. If the domed stadium ever happens, it is doubtful that the X-Men or the Typhoons will play baseball under the roof there.

The Singapore Baseball and Softball Association (SBSA) is not the only such organization in the ASEAN countries. In Malaysia they have teams such as the Vipers and their rivals the Wipers. In Indonesia, for example, you might see the Dobermans. Even in tiny Brunei there is a baseball squad called the Gunners.

By the way, if you are getting transferred to Singapore, and you can play a little baseball, you ought to try out for one of their 8 teams. I don't have all the rosters, but I can tell you that the X-Men have lots and lots of outfielders. What they need are pitchers. If you have a four-seam fastball, I'll bet you could show the hitters for Final Stage, the X-Men's chief rivals, something they haven't seen much of before.

X-RAYS

I was making one of my post-game visits to Emergency, and along with a young doctor I was looking at an X-ray stuck up on the thing that shines light through it. "Oh, no," I expostulated, "This can't be my hand and wrist. There should be a white line across my wrist." All I could see were the white lines suggesting fractures to thumb and fingers. The young doctor assured me that the X-ray had my name and number on it. I began to think that I had taken a head injury as well as the idiot who came into me standing up instead of sliding into the tag I was preparing to put on him right after catching a lovely throw from my catcher on the attempted steal.

While they were putting the plaster and cloth and all that stuff around my hand, I remembered: the white line across my wrist would be in an X-ray of my other arm. Different doctor, different Emergency.

Hey, I just had an idea, I thought of telling the attendant who was waiting for me to relinquish the bed and curtained-off space I was using. When it comes to printing my next collectors' card, maybe I could use a composite X-ray for the picture on the front. Which was kind of dumb, because I didn't have a collector's card until years later, to promote a book called *Baseball Love*.

Okay, I thought a little later, here's another idea. I could put together a book of x-ray pictures, maybe not just the baseball ones. The foot I broke while taking down the school dance decorations from the gym. The hand I broke while punching a wall I didn't know was made of concrete. The nose that got broken by a shoe before it got broken by a baseball and was later broken by a fist and then by a baseball again. The hip that was broken while I was valiantly intervening in a dogfight. The rib I separated while getting boarded in a hockey game in the rink outside McGill University. Then there were the baseball ones, the hand, the wrist, the cracked knee, the occipital.

I guess I could add the laser pictures they sometimes take of the two eyes that have been the end-points of line drives, the X, I guess, that marks the spot. My concussions, one in and one out of baseball, were not photographed, as far as I know. And all the surgical operations, well, that's another story, or maybe another book.

I remember hearing when I was a kid that extended X-ray penetration of your body would have a really bad end result as far as you are concerned. So I used to think back on all my chest X-rays and bone X-rays and try to add up the seconds. In earlier times I would nervously smoke cigarettes while doing this arithmetic. Now I just down endless cups of strong coffee.

And I think of Coleridge's advice to the ball-playing poet: "Make the external internal, the internal X-ternal." Do it fast.

X

There are so many things I miss when I think back to the ways I followed baseball when I was a kid in the far western Canadian sticks. I think I have mentioned the World Series coverage in the October newsreels at the Oliver Theatre, those long black shadows across the newly mown grass at Yankee Stadium in black and white. I've mentioned listening to ball games on the radio. I miss the Look Sharp-da-da-da-da-dah business when you first heard the rustling of the crowd before the game begins, the same song, if that is what it was, that you heard at the Friday night boxing matches.

Another thing I really miss is the newspaper. When I was a kid the Vancouver *Sun* and the Vancouver *Province* took baseball seriously. This was long before the National Hockey League expanded to Vancouver and every other city where ice never forms on back lane puddles. And the National Football League was some semi-amateur affair of constantly moving franchises back east somewhere. When I was a kid it was a thrill to read the baseball pages in the daily paper.

Of course there were the stories of the games the night before, or in my case the night before that, because in the South Okanagan, we read yesterday's Vancouver newspaper. There were the sidebars about hot rookies and grizzled veterans making comebacks. There were the standings to go over with a pencil and the arithmetical skills that your school had prepared you with expressly for this purpose. There were cartoons – car*toons* – of great players, with lots of info tucked around their exaggerated bodies.

And there was the superimposed stuff on the photographs. I had been enamored of this sort of thing earlier, when I was a four-year-old boy sprawled on the living room floor with the opened newspaper, checking out the progress of the Allied troops, turning black Europe into white Europe, with big arrows illustrating the advance of the US Ninth Armored Division eastward toward Berlin, or the islands being hopped in the Pacific, with US or Japanese flags rising from them.

Now there were big arrows on the sports pages. This was true because in the Fifties Mickey Mantle and Frank Howard and Joe Adcock among others were hitting enormous home runs. It was the decade of the sluggers, and there were a lot of cartoons showing guys with prodigious musculature. When the Mick hit one out of Griffith Stadium in 1953, there was a photograph of the left field bleachers, with a superimposed arced arrow showing the ball's path to disappearance over the roof. But when he hit what he considered his biggest blast it was in Yankee Stadium, the house that Ruth built and Mantle tried to demolish. It was May of 1963 when he smote a ball that banged off the facade of the right field roof.

In newspapers all around the continent next day, and in magazines for months afterward, there was a photograph with a wide arrow superimposed on it. At the end of the arrow was a big X right where Mick's home run had smacked the facade. X, I said, wonderingly, marks the spot. The ABCs of baseball are for its young players on their way to whatever level they may reach. The Xs are for lucky guys like Mickey Mantle.

202

XALAPA

I was there only one night in 1964, but I love the city of Xalapa. The University of Vera Cruz is there. The state's symphony is there. The huge and mysterious Olmec heads are there. My friend Willy and I went on a strange pub-crawl there, and I wrote a story about it: "The Xalapa Handkerchief." Like all great cities, it is built on seven hills, and low-level clouds snake their way between them. It is also the home of the Xalapa Chileros.

A lot of people think that Martin Dihigo was the greatest baseball player of all time. He is the only person who is in the baseball halls of fame of the USA, Mexico, Cuba, Venezuela and the Dominican Republic. When he died he was Cuba's national minister of sports. But in 1953 he was the manager of the Xalapa Chileros.

I used to enjoy good conversations with a poet who lived in Xalapa and taught philosophy at the university there. His name is Joaquin Sanchez Macgregor, and when I knew him he had curly brown hair, sort of like a lot of Scotsmen you know. We used to appear in poetry magazines together, as in *El Corno Emplumado* No. 10. He taught philosophy in Cuba during the early years of the revolution there, and returned to take up a job at Veracruz. In the early sixties he was invited to speak at a conference of philosophers at the University of Texas, but he was stopped by the US border police and turned back. He had four counts against him, at least, maybe five: he was a poet, he was a philosopher, he had been to Cuba, and obviously his mother had chosen to become a Mexican. In later years he became a big poobah at the National University (UNAM) in Mexico City. I checked the University of Texas libraries, and sure enough, they have some of his books there. It isn't the hall of fame, but it is, sort of. In Havana and in Xalapa, Joaquin was a big fan of Martin Dihigo.

The Chileros compete in the Veracruz Winter League, the east coast equivalent of the Mexican Pacific League. There are two divisions of five teams each. Xalapa won the championship in 2001–2008.

The 2008–2009 crown was won by the San Andres Tuxtla Sorcerers. They love baseball in the state of Veracruz. Their national dance is a fandango performed in white outfits. Veracruz is a Caribbean nation, you might almost say. If you want to see how much the fans love their Chileros, just go to YouTube and type "Chileros de Xalapa."

Oh, and remember Fernando Valenzuela Jr.? He recently signed with the Chileros as a first baseman and designated hitter.

On second thought, why am I extolling the wonders of Xalapa, my favourite city in Mexico? I know what: you can visit the other towns in the league. I'm sure you'll really like the Córdoba Cafeteros or the Minatitlán Gavilanes. I'll be in Xalapa. You know, going to the symphony.

YAHOOS

My sense is that at a hockey game, or in a bar where people drink and watch hockey games, the majority of the people sitting there and occasionally standing up to spill beer are yahoos. I think that football fans are probably not quite as bad but still leaning toward yahooism. When some clutch of drunken young men is acting badly at the baseball game, I verbally accuse them of being hockey fans, or sometimes football fans. That's why it pains me to admit that at just about any ballpark you will see or hear some yahoos.

In places such as the dome in Toronto, you will see some bozos leaning way out of the front row seats down the foul line, trying to nab a ball that has gone by the bag fair and is thus in play. He is related to the guy who catches a visiting team home run in the stands, throws his arms in the air, turning around and around so the crowd can see how happy he is. I always ask myself why this yahoo is at the game.

I often ask myself why people are at the game if they don't like baseball enough to learn something about the game. Someone on the home team hits a long popup, and a roar goes up from the stands. Why, I ask, do they cheer for an easy out that brings us closer to defeat? I have heard worse: in the top of the ninth inning a hitter for the visiting Eugene Emeralds gets a sacrifice fly to put his team ahead by a run, and nudniks in the Vancouver crowd cheer loudly – presumably because their outfielder caught the ball. I make a point of looking around and loudly wondering where all these Eugene fans came from.

If there's a home team runner on first, and the visiting pitcher throws over there a couple of time, people will boo, and some dimwit will yell, "Play ball!" He has not stopped to think about the score, the number of outs, the count, the record of that runner as a thief, and so on. He has no idea that the pitcher might be checking to see whether the sacrifice bunt is on, or keeping the runner a step closer to first to lower his chances of going to third on a single. That hockey fan in the crowd is missing most of the game. He's the sort of person who complains about baseball's being too "slow." He's more at home at a hockey game, where you don't have to think.

You can be pretty sure that the same guy will join his beer-drinking friends in booing if the opposition gives one of the locals an intentional walk. Why can't baseball be more like my game and my life, he is complaining, where these managers and whatever wouldn't keep doing cowardly things just because they think they're so smart?

You might think that you would be helping these yahoos out if you gave them a book that explains the strategies that are at the heart of the game. But don't delude yourself; these guys don't spend a lot of time reading books.

YANKEES

For years and years I have been wondering how a person could cheer for the New York Yankees. In the Bubba parts of the United States, I have been given to understand, New York is thought to be on the liberal side of things, or as they say down there, "leftist." Wouldn't you think of the New York Yankees as the capitalist centre of the Republican ethos? It was quite a long time ago that Joe E. Lewis said, "Rooting for the Yankees is like rooting for US Steel.

Look at the new Yankee Stadium. In New York they brag about how much it cost to build the thing, billions, more than the entire population of Haiti will earn in the next hundred years. Haiti, where they used to make the baseballs the Yanks toss into the crowd, until China came up with a more economical deal. In Haiti the women who sewed baseballs got a dollar a day. Speaking of the Caribbean, I say that rooting for the Yankees is like rooting for the US Navy.

You know the sneering teenage quarterback parading along the school hall, his minions beside him, his gaze checking out girls, entitlement written all over his face that has never been willingly in front of an opened book? That's the Yankees, I think, and if you are a fan of this team, what are you? Maybe there is some kind of excuse, but I don't see it. I say that rooting for the Yankees in like rooting for DDT.

Who could be more of a New York writer than Jimmy Breslin? He covered the Mets and the Yankees, and he covered lowlife gangsters and high-rise executives. In 1963, in a piece in the *New York Herald Tribune*, he wrote "When you tell the story of this year's American League race ... you go with a little thing called money, because money gets the job done better than all the pride and guts and whatever it is they talk about when an athlete does well." If you are going to root for the New York Yankees, you might as well root for the Bank of America.

If you are a writer or artist or intellectual or wiseacre of some sort, chances are you like baseball, as opposed to the businessmen and smalltime politicians who like football. As we approach the land of clichés, we note that these writers, etc., tend to gravitate toward the Cubs, the Red Sox, the Mets, and maybe still in this late time, the Giants. I have known a few intellectuals who used to like the Yankees because they had grown up as impressionable kids in New York, but as the years of non-addiction went by they learned to embrace the Expos or the Blue Jays or the Mariners. There may be a writer or English prof somewhere who holds a candle for the Bronx Bummers, but I can't figure him or her out. I mean I think that rooting for the Yankees is no better than rooting for whatever taunting strutting team in beautiful uniforms the Bad News Bears were playing.

YARDS

Through the course of the alphabet I have had a few things to say about various ballparks I've been lucky enough to visit. In a much earlier book I published a sequence of prose-like poems called "Yards," about the various parks I'd sat in up to then. In my previous book *Baseball Love* I narrated the first few long baseball road trips my sweetheart and I drove.

I am seldom as excited as I am when we are approaching, say, Oklahoma, and I know that in an hour or two we will be inside Bricktown Ball Park, settling down and watching the RedHawks host the Redbirds. I don't care which part of the park we sit in. If it's a hot day in July I prefer the shade, if there is any. But I like watching baseball from any angle. It's that kind of game, or I'm that kind of fan.

So I would like to make a few remarks, in anything but an organized way, about some of the ballparks I've been in. And I just thought: an awful lot of them have been torn down or deserted by the team that used to play there. Take Tiger Stadium, or Briggs, as I always called it. I have mentioned that it was my first major league park, and that when I was nine years old I was a Tigers fan. I still think that of the many yards I have been in, Tiger Stadium was the one that answered the question: what should the archetypal baseball building look like? The Tigers' home uniforms are the definition of classic, and the park they played in from 1912 to 1999 is the standard from which all other parks decline. The state of Michigan and the USA named it a historical monument, but it was completely demolished in 2009.

My co-pilot Jean is a *connoisseuse* of baseball mascots. She has certain standards. She doesn't care for (with some exceptions) mascots with beaks, and she particularly dislikes the Pittsburgh Pirates Parrot, not just for the beak, but also for the reflexive pun, for the fact that the parrot is dressed as a pirate, etc. She laughed herself silly at the antics of the giant squirrel with the dangerous tail and disappearing feet who used to patrol the Visalia ball field when they were still the Oaks. She was bemused by the Casper mascot, which is not a ghost but a duckbilled platypus named Hobart. But her favourite is Dusty, the whirling mascot of the Tri-City Dust Devils of the Northwest League. She even traded a bunch of our stuff for Dusty's bobble head doll.

I was lucky enough to throw out the first ball at a Milwaukee Brewers home game once, and even luckier to have a seat near the starting post for the famous sausage race, just after they added a fourth sausage. I love it. At first I was browned off when other clubs copied the idea, but then we saw the presidents' race in Washington, and it was pretty neat, those giant Rushmore heads zooming along atop pumping legs. In Atlanta now they have a race of the tools, but it is sponsored by a hardware chain, and that's a little dubious. But my favourite is the race at Nat Bailey Stadium in Vancouver. It is a competition among giant pieces of sushi. We always have bets on the contestants. I have two friends who bet on *Wasabi* at every game, despite the fact that the green blob keeps discovering new ways to lose a big lead and fail miserably. Sort of like the Atlanta Braves.

YAZ

As I think I have mentioned somewhere, the first major league game I ever saw was the first game (and the first inning and a half of the second game) of a double header in Tiger Stadium between Detroit and the Red Sox on July 9th, 1967. Though they would win the AL pennant, on this day the Red Sox were at about .500, and in this first game Tiger pitcher Earl Wilson won his tenth against seven losses, and hit his third home run of the season, a line drive over the left field fence. Dick McAuliffe hit one just below Greg Curnoe and me in the upper deck in right.

Carl Yastrzemski went three for four in this game, but the Tigers won 10–4 in front of 48,000 folks. Apparently he hit a homer in the second game, which the Red Sox won 3–0. Now were are getting to the subject of this piece – things that happened years ago that still nerk me. I'm talking about Carl Yastrzemski's triple crown. There has not been a Triple Crown winner in either league since 1967, and I am glad that it was a Red Sock that got it. I was truly excited that Yaz took Boston to their first pennant in two decades, and that he got the MVP for that year. But.

But why couldn't he have hit home runs in both games of that doubleheader? Then he would not have had to share the home run championship with Harmon Killebrew. The Sox played the Twins in the final series of the season and both sluggers got their 44th dinger in the second last game. In that season-ending doubleheader Yaz went 7 for 8, and the Sox swept to edge the Tigers, who split with the Angels. Why couldn't one more of those hits have been a homer?

Forty some-odd years later, I still gnash my teeth. With one more homer it would have been a clean triple crown. I hate things like that. It still bothers the hell out of me that Ted Williams didn't win the 1954 batting championship because he was penalized for being walked so often. Bobby Avila had a lower batting average, but won because the rules still specified official at-bats instead of plate appearances, which became the rule a little too late. Williams would have had enough at-bats, too, if he hadn't broken his collarbone in spring training.

A lot of things gripe me about Ted Williams' bad luck. How many home runs would he have amassed if he hadn't gone off flying fighter planes during two wars? Or what about this one? What if he had swung at a ball an inch off the plate and got one more hit in 1949? Then he would have won his third triple crown. I liked George Kell all right, but somewhere inside me I still harbour a little hope that a recount would reverse the horribly annoying batting average stats for that year: Kell .3429, Williams .3428.

Happily, the opposite happens from time to time. On September

30, 1972, Roberto Clemente got his 3000th and last regular season hit, then died in a plane that was trying to take aid supplies to earthquake-stricken Nicaragua.

And those awful things that never fade into the past happen outside of baseball too. Remember the hanging chads in Florida during the US presidential vote of 2000? You remember, the one in which more US Americans voted for Al Gore than for George W. Bush?

YUNIESKY

It used to be that Cuban ballplayers had first names like Tony and Orlando and Sandy. Not any more. I don't know whether it's true about Cuban society as a whole, but in recent years Cuban baseball is full of weird non-traditional first names. You might have expected some Russian names such as Vladimir and Alexie, and there have been a few, but you are more likely to get Vicyohandri or Eliecer.

But most of them start with Y. It is as if all the Cuban mothers between 1975 and 1985 got into a national contest to give their sons the most peculiar and un-Spanish names they could find with a Y in front. While Black mothers in the USA were naming their kids Raeshawon and Dawntrelle, Cuban *madres* chose appellations such as Yorelvis and Yoandry. When someone shouts "Yo!" they all turn around.

Just about everyone knows the story of infielder Yuniesky Betancourt, the *gusano* who was traded in 2009 from the Seattle Mariners to the Kansas City Royals because he was such a pain in the ass. In his few years in the American League he has had the lowest walk percentage and lowest on-base percentage in the American League. He doesn't have a good work ethic, as they say, and so he doesn't get along well with his bosses, either. In Seattle he once said that Mariners manager Don Wakamatsu was worse than Fidel Castro. The Mariners traded him for a guy that posts Internet pictures of himself asleep on the toilet.

Another infielder is *gusano* Yunel Escobar, who works for the Toronto Blue Jays. Like Betancourt, he was born in 1982. Unlike Betancourt, he has discipline at the plate, resulting in a good number of walks for a middle infielder, and a satisfactory on-base percentage. For some reason the Atlanta Braves ditched him. Maybe they didn't like the Cuban music on his website.

The Pirates have a pitcher from Pinar del Rio named Yoslin Herrera, who gave up 35 hits in 18.1 innings in 2008, then was outrighted to Triple-A Indianapolis. But most of the youngsters whose names start with Y are still playing in Cuba, where there aren't any millionaire brats.

Yovany Aragon played for the gold-medal Cuban team in the 2000 Sydney Olympics. Yorelvis Charles is a slugging third baseman for the lowly Ciego de Ávila Tigers, In 2005–06 he batted in 72 runs in 90 games. Yobal Dueñas defected to the Yankees, but was arrested in South Carolina for stealing jewelry. Yasser Gómez and Yadel Martí were kicked off the Cuban national team because they were looking for a chance to desert. Yuliesky Gurriel, a third baseman for Sancti Spiritus, is currently considered the best player in Cuba, and has US-American scouts drooling and dangling moolah. There were even news stories planted that he had defected in Colombia, but he has gone on record as saying that he doesn't want to.

Yadier Pedroso and Yulieski González are two young pitchers who anchor the Havana nine that is always a force to be reckoned with. Of course their task is made a lot simpler by the powerful left fielder Yoandry Urgellés, who his .366 when he was 24 years old.

Of course, there are more youngsters coming up all the time. The baseball talent in Cuba is inexhaustible, no matter how many dollars are flashed by the Gringos. Keep an eye out, for example, on Yoandy Garlobo, Yunieski Maya and Yosvani Pérez. In Cuba the Ys have it.

ZAUN

My wife has a heart for catchers.

But last night when she saw Gregg Zaun analyzing the American League Championship Series game 6 between the Yankees and the Angels, she disapproved of the outfit Gregg was wearing, a checked shirt with a striped vest, and longish hair jelled back. I said that I thought he looked pretty good. Jean gave me that look that signifies that I am so out of it. But I could see that she was scolding Gregg indulgently. She just can't resist catchers.

When Jean acquired her fantasy team for 2004, she inherited a last-place finisher, so she got to get the number one draft. Pudge Rodriguez was on the list because someone didn't protect him, but this was the winter when everyone was buzzing about Kazuo Matsui. He was the hottest prospect since Jackie Jensen, or maybe Napoleon Bonaparte. Oh, you lucky person sitting in the catbird seat, all the other owners said to Jean, you get to pick Kaz Matsui, the greatest thing since two-sided Scotch tape. So Jean, feeling a little leery about it, chose Kaz. He hit a home run over the center field fence in his first major league at-bat. But he did not burn up the league. He batted .272, which average he has kept up since, while Pudge hit .334, his highest number ever. Now he is headed for the Hall of Fame.

To this day, Jean can be heard from time to time whimpering "Pudge."

And what about Benito Santiago? He's been nowhere for years, but she loved him when he was a middle-aged bullpen pitcher for the Kansas City Royals a couple of years ago. You'd better not say anything bad about Benito, even if you are the steroid cops. My friend Jack is lucky that he lives way back in Buffalo, because he likes to call Santiago "Windshield Man," alluding to a notorious car crash in Florida that cost him most of the 1988 season. Santiago is the only catcher to lead his league in passed balls and errors and still win the Golden Glove award.

The real reason Jean favours him and I'm jealous? Jean says he still has the best butt in baseball, and in terms of body-type he is pretty well my opposite.

But what explains her attraction to Bob Brenly? She won't say, exactly. I'm thinking the mustache, although I have to remind myself that she usually bugs me to shave mine off if I have one on. I do know that she often brings back that wonderful scene in the bottom of the ninth in the seventh game of the 2001 World Series, when the Diamondbacks got to Mariano Duncan and the game was over and Derek Jeter was sitting there in the dugout with utter disbelief on his entitlement face, and Brenly's guys had beaten the New York Yankees and someone had to pack up all those Yankee ws champion hats and ship them to an African village. And now if I am listening to a Cubs game and Jean hears Brenly's voice, she comes into the TV room for an inning or two.

However, I'm not really worried. My father was a catcher. My mother was a catcher. In the summer of my sixteenth year I was a catcher. Jean must be able to sense the vibes. I can't get her to call me "Pudge," though.

ZEPHYRS

I don't know exactly how my Kosmic League team got the name Granville Grange Zephyrs. I don't know who gave us the name. It's unlikely that they knew about the Denver Zephyrs. In 1971, when the Kosmic League began, the Denver team was still the Bears. They became the Zephyrs, named after a famous passenger train, in 1985. I remember seeing a picture of a guy in a uniform that was Bears on one side and Zephyrs on the other. In 1993 the Zephyrs, with their green and black colours intact, relocated in New Orleans. You know – in the Pacific Coast League. Just as there had been a Zephyr train in Colorado, there was a famous Zephyr rollercoaster in New Orleans.

I also doubt that the team was named after Zephyrus. As anyone reading Percy Bysshe Shelley or Sheila Watson will know, the ancient Greeks just naturally understood the seasons and weather in terms of gods. The four winds were associated with seasons, and of course the most gentle one, Zephyrus the west wind, is responsible for spring. He was the father of fruit and flowers, and was always making love with someone, his five wives, his mistresses, the earth itself. He was also in love with a lad named Hyacinth, and when Hyacinth went off with Apollo, Zephyrus managed to get Hyacinth killed by a discus he had been throwing. The wind blew it back the way the wind takes a would-be homer back onto the field at Coors Field in Denver.

Actually, this is all beginning to sound a little like Vancouver. But I wonder. The Granville Grange was under the Granville Street Bridge, on the approach to hip Granville Island. It was the studio for some sculptors who were then working in fiberglass, one of those sculptors being our first baseman Scoop Toppings. Toppings died of fiberglass inhalation after our second season, leaving me as our oldest player.

I liked our name even though I didn't make it up. I made up a few *noms de baseball* for the league's players, and even one team name. But I didn't make up Zephyrs, and I don't know for sure whether I was the first to refer to us as the Zeds. Let Oakland have the A's, we said; we are the Zeds. It was a perfectly hip and Kosmic thing to do, and so much better than Zees would have been, eh? We had sticky labels made up with the white letters ZED on black background. We wore these on our caps and sometimes our foreheads.

215

Last in the alphabet – first in your hearts, we said. Zeds Blow Early Lead, said the sports page of the *Georgia Straight*. Who's he, asks an infielder for the Afghani Oil Kings. Apollo made the flowering hyacinth with his blood, said some poet in our outfield.

ZIMMER

It's the German word for room, but any baseball aficionado knows that it stands for the short fat manager/coach guy that Bill Lee called "the designated gerbil." He is in that group of major leaguers who look funny and are expected to give sportswriters funny remarks to quote. If they don't, of course, the sportswriters will think of something funny they should have said. Think Yogi Berra. Think John Kruk. Think Casey Stengel.

Don Zimmer was a purported 5'9" infielder in the National League from 1954 to 1963, and then a Washington Senator for a couple years before going to play in Japan. Most people think that he had a metal plate in his skull, but in fact, after a bad beaning in the minors, the doctors drilled four holes in his head and later filled them with a miracle substance. It didn't do much for his hitting. His lifetime batting average was .235, but somehow he was picked for the All-Star team in 1961, a year in which he wound up with an OPS of .694. It wasn't just because of the rule that says that each team had to send a player; the Cubs also placed .300-hitting George Altman. Maybe it was because one of the two games was played at Wrigley.

But we don't really remember Don Zimmer as a player. We picture him as an older guy sitting in the dugout, the middle of his body surrounded by a 45-inch belt. He was manager of the year with the Cubbies in 1989, winning the National League East before bowing to the Giants in five games. It was, I guess, the highlight of Zimmer's career, unless you count coming in second in a mixed martial arts bout with Pedro Martinez in an October game in 2003. Pedro grabbed the round bald head of the charging 72-year-old guy they used to call

Popeye, and flung him to the ground. Zim's Yankees won the game, but the Red Sox took the ALCS series in a highly emotional and alcoholic comeback.

Once back in 1989, Zimmer was asked about the Cubs-Cardinals rivalry. "All you see in Red Sox-Yankees games are fights and cops dragging people out by the hair," said the hairless gerbil. "You rarely see fights here. These are nice people."

Zimmer has dressed as a coach with the Expos, the Padres, the Red Sox, the Yankees again, the Cubs, the Giants, the Red Sox again, the Rockies, and the Yankees yet again. He was a manager for Knoxville, Buffalo, Indianapolis, Key West and Salt Lake City. In the majors he managed the Padres, Red Sox, Rangers, and the Cubs. When it got to be so that no photographer could be found who would agree to photograph him in a baseball uniform, he went to Tampa Bay Devil Rays to be an "executive advisor."

Don't, he told manager Joe Madden, charge the mound when Pedro's up there.

ZOO

It's curious to me that there are some ballparks that get nicknames and others that don't. There are probably local nicknames that don't get out to the edges of civilization where I reside, but really? Does that monstrosity in St. Petersburg have a nickname you can print in a family book such as this? It's called "The Trop," of course, and maybe that is better than Tropicana Field. I mean how can you call some badly coloured artificial turf under a concrete dome a "field"? No wonder hardly anyone goes to games there, even when the team wins the American League pennant. I mean they can stay outside and watch dead pelicans fall from the sky around the old Raytheon Corp. plant.

Remember The House that Ruth Built? That's the name that the pro-business reporters used to refer to the heap of toxic waste next to the new 500 billion dollar Yankee Stadium, the house that dollars built. Perhaps because New York is so nice you have to say it twice, the building earned a number of nicknames. One of the sweetest was "The Bronx Zoo." This is a reference not to the catcher that used to squat there, but to the humanoids that filled its seats and wandered its smelly concourse. A typical day at the zoo is captured in a wonderful book called *Yo-Yos with Money* (New York, United Artists, 1979) in which poets and Mets fans Ted Berrigan and Harris Schiff attend a Red Sox game at Yankee Stadium with a tape recorder. The transcribed book prints everything the tape recorder could hear, for instance the loud boos when the PA announces that the National Anthem will be rendered by the Boston Pops Orchestra. The dialog of Schiff and Berrigan is what you might expect from a couple of bent New York poets, and the reports of fistfights in the crowd are terse.

When Wrigley Field was famously dubbed "The Friendly Confines," the phrase was first meant to suggest a haven for the road-weary Cubbies, but has come to suggest the nine-inning party in the bleachers, where utter strangers pay the kid with the portable spritz-fan a dollar per face-spray, and the motorcycle gang boyos tell you why they are drinking mai-tais instead of beer (because you get the same-sized plastic mug for the same price). Meanwhile a picnic spreads from a family of five until it encompasses the left-centre field bleachers as far as the eye cares to see. You don't have to buy a pennant-winning team to have fun.

If I may, I would like to address a question to the fans of the Los Angeles Dodgers. You know – those folks who arrive at Dodgers Stadium in the third inning and leave after the seventh. If you are going to refer to the site as Chavez Ravine, why do you pronounce it "ShavEZ" instead of the way the millions of Mexicans around you do?

Oh, and here is a note for those US Americans who might have wondered why the Montreal Expos' edifice was called "The Big Owe." Some newspaper type called it the Big O, suggesting both its shape and the fact that it had been the principal site for the 1976 Olympics.

As you know, Olympics construction always costs 20 times as much as the promoters tell the taxpayers that it will. Mayor Drapeau promised that the Olympics had as much chance of running a deficit as a man had of getting pregnant. Long long after the Games had gone and the Expos had come and gone, the pregnant Montreal taxpayers were paying for the crumbling heap with the roof that never did work.

The Expos are now in a new stadium in Washington, where fiscal responsibility rules the day.

ZWILLING

I guess everyone knows that Henry Aaron is first in major league baseball when it comes to alphabetical order. That's one thing the steroid boys aren't going to take away from him unless they come up with a juiced aardvark. But how many people know whose name is last in the *Official Encyclopedia of Baseball*?

Let's see a show of hands for Dutch Zwilling.

Edward Harrison Zwilling was five foot six and weighed 160 pounds, pretty common for the early days of the twentieth century. He was one of two players on the 1910 Chicago White Sox roster whose names started with Z, the other being Rollie Zeider. Zwilling was a 21-year-old left-handed outfielder who had 100 plate appearances that year, and batted .184. He got hit by a pitch once, made one sacrifice bunt, and stole one base. Then he disappeared from the major league scene for a few years. If you know where he went, tell me.

In 1914 he was back in the majors with the Chicago Whales of the Federal League and so was Rollie Zeider, a utility infielder and right-handed hitter. With the Whales Dutch was a slugger, with an OPS over .800 for two years. His 16 home runs led the Federal League in 1914, and in 1915 he led the league in RBIs with 94. When the Federal League was forced to quit after that year, Dutch was its all-time homer king with 29.

The Whales had a terrific new baseball stadium called Weeghman Park, so in 1916 the Chicago Cubs welcomed a merger with the Whales, so that they could play in that venue, which became known as Wrigley Field. Dutch Zwilling and Rollie Zeider both went over to the Cubs, thus becoming the only two players to wear all three Chicago uniforms. The Cubs had a third Z man in third baseman Heinie Zimmerman, who was a much better hitter than either of them, but who would get traded to the Giants and then implicated in the Black Sox scandal, but that's another story.

Dutch was mainly a pinch hitter for the Cubs, and got only 53 at bats in 35 games in 1916. The Cubs were not a powerhouse; they finished fifth, 26.5 games behind Brooklyn. You would have thought that the young outfielder who hit all those extra-base hits in the park over the past two years would have made the transition to the National League, but he hit just one homer, and after 1916 he never played another big league game.

He was still around for a long time, though. He managed in the minors, mostly in the American Association, coached for a year at Cleveland, and went on to work as a scout for the New York Yankees and Mets. He was connected with major league baseball for over 60 years. He died at age 89 in 1978. And now that it looks as if Andrew Zwirchitz has finished his career in the independent Atlantic league and isn't going to get called up, Dutch Zwilling is still the last guy in the Baseball Encyclopedia, not to mention the book you have just finished reading.

ENDNOTES:

"A" – 1949 cap of the Almendares Alacranes of the old Cuban League, which existed from 1878 to 1961.
"B" – 1940 cap of the Joe Louis Brown Bombers, a black semi-pro team that competed in an otherwise all-white independent Colorado Springs league from late 1940s to early 1950s.

"C" – 1915 Chicago Whales cap, a team of the Federal League from 1914 to 1915.

"D" – 1933 Davenport Blue Sox cap, then of the Mississippi League, its home field at Davenport, Iowa.

"E" – 1957 cap of the Eugene Emeralds™ of Eugene, Oregon, charter member of the Northwest League,™ a historic mark of a Minor League Baseball® team based in Eugene, Oregon.

"F" – Cal State Fullerton Titans cap, College. http://www.fullertontitans.com

"G" – Official Home On-Field cap for the Winnipeg Goldeyes, formerly with the Northern League. Beginning in 2011, the team will be a member of the American Association of Independent Professional Baseball. Winnipeg MB www.goldeyes.com

"H" – 1931 Homestead Grays cap. The team was part of the Negro League, home field in Homestead PA.

"I" – Official cap for the Fighting Illini, the University of Illinois team, member of the Big Ten Conference. http://www.fightingillini.com/sports/m-basebl/ill-m-basebl-body.html

"J" – Official Home cap for the Jacksonville Suns™ of the Double-A Southern League,™ a Minor League Baseball® team based in Jacksonville, Florida and Double-A™ affiliate of the Florida Marlins. More information can be found at www.jaxsuns.com

"K" – Official Home Cap for the Kannapolis Intimidators™ of the South Atlantic League,™ a Minor League Baseball® team based in Kannapolis, North Carolina and a Single-A™ affiliate of the Chicago White Sox. More information can be found at www.intimidatorsbaseball.com

"L" – Lancaster Barnstormers of Pennsylvania play in the independent Atlantic League. www.lancasterbarnstormers.com

"M" – Mudville Nine,™ of the California League,™ a historic mark of a Minor League Baseball® team that was based in Stockton, California. Mudville Nine, a name taken from "Casey at the Bat," has graced more than one team in recent times. The Stockton Ports™ of the Single-A™ California League™ went as the Mudville Nine in 2000-2001.

"N" – 1947 cap of the Newark Bears, formerly of the Atlantic League, joined the independent Canadian-American League in 2011.

"O" – 1950 cap of the Oakland Oaks™ of the Pacific Coast League,™ a historic mark of a Triple-A™ Minor League Baseball® team that was based in Oakland, California. After 1955 the team moved to Vancouver, British Columbia where it became the Vancouver Mounties.™

"P" – 1958 cap of the Phoenix Giants™ of the Pacific Coast League™, a historic mark of a Triple-A™ Minor League Baseball® team that was based in Pheonix Arizona.

The Pheonix Giants were a Pacific Coast League affiliate of the San Francisco Giants from 1958 to 1986, except for the years 1960-1965, when they were in Tacoma, Washington.

"Q" – Quebec Capitals of the independent Can-Am League, successor of the Northeast League. www.capitalesdequebec.com

"R" – Seattle Rainiers™ of the Pacific Coast League,™ a historic mark of a Triple-A™ Minor League Baseball® team that was based in Seattle, Washington. This team began as the Seattle Angels™ in the Triple-A Pacific Coast League, and were disbanded after the 1968 season to make room for the American League's Seattle Pilots. 1955 cap.

"S" – Santurce Cangrejeros, founded in 1939, and reborn a number of times, have been the most successful team in Puerto Rico. 1954 cap.

"T" – Tampa Tarpons™ of the Florida State League,™ a historic mark of a Single-A™ Minor League Baseball® team that was based in Tampa, Florida. This team originally played in the Class D, and then later played for the Single-A Florida State League.

"U" – Utica Braves™ of the Eastern League,™ a historic mark of a Double-A™ Minor League Baseball® team that was based in Utica, New York. This team played in the Can-Am League and the Eastern League from 1939 till 1943.

"V" – Official Home cap for the Salem-Keizer Volcanoes™ of the Northwest League,™ a Minor League Baseball® team based in Keizer, Oregon and a Short-Season/Single-A™ affiliate of the San Francisco Giants. More information can be found at www.volcanoesbaseball.com

"W" – 1970 cap of the Winnipeg Whips™ of the International League,™ a historic mark of a Triple-A™ Minor League Baseball® team that was based in Winnipeg. In 1970 the Buffalo Bisons™ team was moved to Winnipeg and was renamed the Whips. The team had a brief, unsuccessful run before being moved to Hampton Roads, Virginia.

"X" – Xalapa Chileros play in the Veracruz winter league.

"Y" – York White Roses™, a historic mark of a Minor League Baseball® team that operated in several leagues between 1894 and 1969.

"Z" – Official Home Cap for the New Orleans Zephyrs™ of the Pacific Coast League,™ a Minor League Baseball® team based in Metairie, Louisiana and a Triple-A™ affiliate of the Florida Marlins. Formerly of Denver, Colorado. More information can be found at www.zephyrsbaseball.com

The publisher would like to thank Minor League Baseball for their kind permission to reproduce caps found in this book.

www.minorleaguebaseball.com

COLOPHON

Manufactured spring 2011 by BookThug in an edition of 500 copies.
Distributed in Canada by the Literary Press Group: www.lpg.ca
Distributed in the USA by Small Press Distribution: www.spdbooks.org
Shop on-line at www.bookthug.ca

Type+Design: www.beautifuloutlaw.com